Liberal Clichés
And Conservative
Solutions

Liberal Clichés And Conservative Solutions

Edited
by
Hon. Philip M. Crane

Green Hill Publishers
Ottawa, Illinois

Liberal Clichés and Conservative Solutions

© 1984 by Green Hill Publishers, Inc.
All Rights Reserved. No part of this book may be used or
reproduced in any manner without written permission, except in
the case of brief quotations embodied in critical reviews.

Copies of this book may be purchased directly from the publisher
for $3.95. All inquiries should be addressed to Green Hill
Publishers, Inc., 722 Columbus St., Ottawa, IL 61350. (815) 434-
7905.

Printed in the United States of America.

ISBN: 0-89803-147-8

Contents

Acknowledgments

The Republican Study Committee is a team of conservative members of Congress that pools its resources to generate more effective research, legislation, and media coverage. The RSC's chairman in 1984 is Bill Dannemeyer of California.

RSC members and staff are loyal Republicans and strong conservatives. Along with the majority of our fellow citizens, we believe in a secure, fiscally responsible, and opportunity-rich America. And we fight for that vision every day.

This book is part of that fight. It represents the attempt of sixteen rank-and-file public servants to clear the air of liberal disinformation, and contains dozens of new ways to improve the lives of individual Americans and their families. We address education, deficits, the prevention of nuclear war, and many other issues.

I want to express my thanks to Frank Gregorsky of the RSC staff. Frank is responsible for much of the staff work that produced *Liberal Clichés and Conservative Solutions*. I'd also like to thank Jameson Campaigne and Richard Wheeler of Green Hill for their unfailing cooperation and upbeat spirits throughout the book's preparation.

PHILIP M. CRANE
Immediate Past Chairman
Republican Study Committee

Introduction
Completing the Revolution

By Jack Kemp, MC

Ideas have consequences. Good ideas have good consequences, bad ideas bad consequences. As both the Old and New Testaments tell us, a good tree cannot bear bad fruit, nor can a bad tree bear good fruit.

The American people have been saddled with liberal-left policies off and on for decades. Liberal-left philosophy reached its zenith in the Carter-Mondale administration. What were its results?

Domestically: skyrocketing inflation, record-high interest rates, rising joblessness, shrinking capital stock, social discontent, and tensions among groups seeking political power and privilege by trying to divide an economic pie they thought could no longer expand in an "era of limits."

Internationally: collapsing respect for America, U.S. officials held hostage by weak nations and terrorist outlaws, brazen global aggression by the Soviet empire, a sagging national defense structure, and the democratic West on the defensive with no leader.

The product of liberal-left policies was national decline on every front. "By their fruits you shall know them."

When you examine the attitudes underlying liberal and conservative policies today, you can't help concluding that liberal-left policy is *elitist,* conservative and neoconservative policy *populist.*

Elitism is a recurring threat in American politics. Indeed, it is a permanent danger in every democratic society.

Elitism always makes its appearance as an attack on the American people's faith in democratic principles. That is why, five years before the U.S. Constitution was written, America's Founding Father, Thomas Jefferson, wrote, "Every government degenerates when trusted to the rulers of the people alone. The people themselves therefore are its only safe depositories."

Sometimes in our past, elitists have tried to suppress freedom of speech and press; sometimes they stymied popular electoral decisions; once they were proslavery; they have supported international financial and corporate interests at the expense of open democratic competition. Elitists don't trust people to govern or control themselves.

Today, during a transition in the early phase of the populist Reagan revolution, elitism appears in defense of the status quo.

Defeatism and apology are hallmarks of liberal-left Democrats today. "Don't change anything, don't reduce tax rates on American workers, don't deregulate and cut down bureaucracy, don't restrain federal spending, don't touch the Supreme Court or revitalize the Civil Rights Commission, don't modernize our national defense, don't react when the Soviet empire shoots down commercial jetliners carrying U.S. congressmen, don't defend U.S. interests anywhere in the world, freeze every weapon in sight, and above all, please don't upset the 'doves' in the Kremlin."

If defending the status quo is a standpatter's attitude, the liberal-left Democrat is the standpatter par excellence.

Liberalism did not always defend things as they are. During FDR's, Truman's, and John Kennedy's administrations, liberal policies did have progressive and populist goals. They attempted to secure the rights of the common man against the elites of their day. Centrist Democratic presidents through Kennedy always remembered that prosperity and democracy were linked.

Old-guard Republicans as well as modern liberals should be reminded that not one prewar Roosevelt budget absorbed more than 10.6 percent of the gross national product, and all the New Deal budgets during the twelve-year term, including World War II, averaged only 19.1 percent of GNP. The current budget, by contrast, is projected to expend 24 percent of GNP. By this measure, FDR's New Deal seems like the golden age of conservative government.

Roosevelt's latter-day successors have forgotten what made the Democratic party so popular in the 1930s. By the last decade, elitist liberals grew tired of the deliberative process of democratic legislation. They not only short-circuited the legislature by appealing to the courts and agencies to force their agenda on an unwilling public, but even turned against the populist economic policies they used to support.

For example, deep reductions in personal income-tax rates were proposed by the Kennedy administration in 1963; yet liberal Democrats attacked similar populist tax cuts offered by Senator Bill Roth and myself in the late 1970s. Reducing tariff and nontariff barriers (a policy known as the "Kennedy round") and liberalizing international trade to create American jobs had been a cornerstone of President Kennedy's economic program; our liberals are pushing protectionism, a policy dear to the hearts of big corporate managers.

In a phrase, nothing is clearer than the domestic and foreign-policy *defeatism* infecting liberal Democrats today.

Whenever some political leaders excuse their paralysis by complaining that they can't do anything to solve problems, the American people's answer is to elect others who *can*.

Thus the voters began a revolution in 1980 by turning out the Carter-Mondale administration and electing Ronald Reagan, a Republican-controlled Senate, and a stronger GOP minority in the House.

We House Republicans, naturally, have been in a precarious situation, our power to introduce and amend legislation increasingly circumscribed by unfair rules imposed by Speaker Tip O'Neill and the Democratic majority's leaders.

Still, within these constraints, the Republicans have pushed reforms in legislative initiatives and in floor debates.

As chairman of the House Republican Conference, I'm proud of the quality and depth of the work of our Republican congressmen, fifteen of whom are represented in the chapters of this book.

The 1980 election *was* "a new beginning"—but the Reagan revolution remains to be completed. Plainly, this cannot happen until President Reagan has a GOP-controlled Senate *and* House to forge the legislative program we need to finish the conservative agenda described in this book.

In the domestic area, our agenda includes:

- Passing a constitutional amendment to allow voluntary prayer by public school children, a right supported by huge majorities of the electorate, including 80 percent of Democrats.
- Restraining and overhauling the still growing federal budget, which continues to be excessive because

Democratic leaders control the House, where budget measures constitutionally begin.

- New tax reforms involving simplification and rate reduction, in the form of a flat income-tax rate.
- Educational reforms to restore the basics of education—such as math skills and verbal literacy—to strengthen discipline, and to return primary control of children's schooling to parents at the local level.
- Passing a constructive, progressive bill to establish urban enterprise zones to help put our people to work in productive, meaningful jobs in our inner cities and other depressed areas.
- Reform of housing programs to increase the stake of the dependent poor in their housing, and to make basic housing once again affordable and available.
- Passage of appropriate legislation to remove any doubt that the human rights proclaimed in the Declaration of Independence extend to all human beings. Just as the Thirteenth Amendment recognized the civil rights of blacks who had been forced into slavery, the "peculiar institution" of the last century, so must we guarantee the full constitutional rights of the unborn who are subject to the peculiar institution of our age, abortion.

In the areas of national defense and foreign policy, the conservative agenda includes:

- Modernizing and streamlining our entire defense structure to increase its deterrent capability against nuclear threat and our military preparedness in the face of dangers of conventional warfare around the world.
- Establishing a comprehensive strategy, following recommendations by the National Bipartisan Commission on Central America, to protect the Western Hemisphere against Soviet- and Cuban-inspired

aggression, and to promote prosperity from Cape Horn to the Arctic.

- Supporting the worldwide popular demand, both outside and within the Iron Curtain countries, for democratic reform, basic natural rights, and economic growth. (To give just one example, the U.S. must insist upon the solemn commitment given by Stalin to hold democratic elections in Poland. That promise was the principle behind the Helsinki accords, and we cannot let those confined within the Soviet empire think we have forgotten it.)

To this agenda I would add one item, which, in a sense, is the necessary condition for all the others: monetary reform. In the long run, achieving any of these goals will be far more difficult if they are not accompanied by sustained, worldwide, noninflationary economic prosperity, which offers the hope of a rising standard of living.

In a stagnant economy, share-the-wealth schemes advanced by liberal redistributionists become speciously attractive. Small is of necessity beautiful when the economy is shrinking and people's hopes are being shattered by material want. The only way to get those schemes off the board is to create the conditions for genuine prosperity.

Without doubt, the *Reagan budget and tax reforms laid the foundation for this kind of growth*. That was demonstrated by the strong recovery of the U.S. economy in 1983, which confounded the predictions of most liberal economic "experts." But proper fiscal policy alone is not sufficient, for two reasons.

First, inflation is a decline in the value of money, and so it can only be cured by proper monetary policy. Second, improper monetary policy can largely offset the good effects of proper fiscal policy. This was clearly shown by the secondary drop in the economy in 1982, which did not give way to recovery until monetary policy was corrected.

Several things can be done right now to reduce this problem. For example, the nation's central bank, the Federal Reserve, should stop trying to do the impossible—control the *quantity* of money. Instead, it should stabilize money's value in regard to the *things money can buy*.

Nearly every important decision about the well-being of American families concerns the *value* of money: new work responsibilities, a new job, saving for the children's education or for retirement, taking out a loan for a new home or car.

Thus monetary policy is an issue of *justice* between borrowers and lenders, workers and employers, the past, present, and future. So it is not surprising that honest money is also a blue-collar, middle-class, populist, bread-and-butter issue.

We conservatives well remember that our party dominated U.S. politics for seventy-two years, over a third of our constitutional history. Our majority stemmed from policies informed by Lincoln's teaching that the morality of our revolution against Britain lay in our commitment to equality and liberty.

During the GOP's long predominance, Republican policies were rooted in the central idea of the Declaration of Independence, the idea of enlightened popular consent to a government that protects human rights.

From that central idea, the Republican party:

- Fashioned a strong, nonbureaucratized federal government against sectionalism;
- Supported robust economic growth through low taxes and a stable gold dollar;
- Encouraged millions of the world's poor and oppressed to immigrate here and share the blessings of freedom;

- Extended civil rights to newly emancipated blacks;
- Stimulated the building of a national railroad system to restore national unity after the Civil War;
- Projected an unchallengeable navy around the world;
- Negotiated arms-control agreements to limit the size of the world's naval fleets.

As certainly as Lincoln's party swept the political field in the 1860s, today's conservative Republicans can complete the revolution the American people began in 1980.

The conservative Republicans represented in this book have restored the idea of enlightened popular consent respecting basic human rights to its central place in policymaking. For us, the moral principles of freedom and democracy are universal truths and dependable guides for all people everywhere.

We don't doubt that the demands of equality and liberty impose a great burden on the American people. We are obligated to extend their liberating influence—to protect the needy within our own society, to support freedom throughout the world, and to encourage hope in the darkest Siberian corners of the Soviet empire.

Americans expect their government to transform these truths into realities.

The following chapters will indicate how we propose to do that.

The Cliché

"Republican talk is profamily but Republican deeds are antichildren."

The Republican party's concern for life seems to begin at conception and end at birth. Republicans cut child nutrition programs. They oppose federally subsidized day-care centers that would help working mothers. They oppose sex education and birth-control training, and the result is more unwanted children and abortions. Republicans who praise the family really just want to cut budgets and control other people's morality.

1

What Really Helps Families?

By Tom Bliley, MC

In the last twenty-five years the federal government's assault on the American family has taken on warlike dimensions. Policies and programs designed to help and encourage have tended to hurt and destroy. A Democratic-controlled Congress has pulled and tugged at the moral fabric holding together our families, and now that that fabric is torn and weakened, liberals are trying to blame somebody else, anybody else, for the destruction of lives and relationships.

Never before have the people of our country experienced such disastrous consequences from misguided government policy. Illegitimate births, single-parent families, teenage pregnancies, child abuse, and domestic violence have increased drastically in the face of billions of federal dollars spent "to fight the problem."

If Republicans are to blame, they should be blamed for failing to stop policies that give birth to a moral catastrophe. If Republicans are to blame, they should be blamed for failing to bring positive, constructive solutions before the American people.

We are, indeed, engaged in a war. But it's not a budget-cutting war, or a war to "control morality." This is a war to save life, to preserve the family, and to protect our children.

This war involves two different ideas about what it means to help families. One side says the way to help is to assist families to perform on their own *as* families and to care for their own members. The other side believes the way to help is to relieve families of the burden of caring for themselves and to lay that burden on the government.

Republicans have generally been in favor of letting families take care of themselves, except in extreme cases where a family is not capable of helping itself. Liberal-backed federal welfare programs have been based on the other approach, and Democrats have broadened federal programs to include more and more family responsibilities. It's no secret that the Democratic strategy is achieving its goals and gaining momentum.

But that greater momentum is resulting in the increasing weakness of the American family, and that weakness means that America is in danger of crumbling on its own foundation.

The family is the basic building block of our society, and it functions in a unique way to nurture and strengthen its members. If we cripple the family, we cripple a nation.

Republicans believe that there is no replacement for the family and its functions and that many government programs threaten its existence. An example of this was found in an experiment by the Department of Health, Education, and Welfare in the 1970s. Tests in Denver and Seattle showed that *families with incomes guaranteed by the government were falling apart at a rate 60 percent higher than families receiving only supplemental benefits.*

In other words, many husbands and fathers left their families when they realized they were no longer needed for financial support. In the end, the only thing that the guaranteed income guaranteed for many families was long-term dependence on the welfare system and short-term marriages.

The same kind of problem exists with the federal welfare program, Aid to Families with Dependent Children (AFDC). Although many AFDC recipients stay in the program for less than two years, as many as 20 percent of the recipients use about 60 percent of the total benefits available under the program.

In some respects, they're hooked on the welfare system and they don't know how to break the habit.

Because of these kinds of problems, Republicans have been wary of any program that tends to destroy the nurturing quality of family life. Republicans oppose nutrition assistance to children when the assistance is made available *only* if the child eats his three meals a day away from home. We want to see children well-fed and healthy, and we also want them to *enjoy meals with their families at home,* not with the social worker at the corner cafeteria.

Republicans also oppose child-care benefits which go *only*

to families who choose to send their children out to professional day-care centers. Some families should get federal assistance if they choose to care for their children at home.

And Republicans oppose family-planning and sex-education programs which encourage experimentation and sexual activity among our children. Parents spend years trying to teach their children the difference between right and wrong, and then have these efforts undermined by a sex-education plumbing specialist who says there is no difference between right and wrong.

Sex-education and family-planning programs should emphasize the importance of the family, not destroy its very foundations.

Unfortunately, opposition to these programs makes people think Republicans, especially conservatives, are really interested only in cutting budgets. People imagine that Republicans sit around all the time saying, "So what if the poor suffer. We've saved a couple of bucks and kept taxes down for the middle class. It's a matter of priorities, and poor kids just aren't high on the list."

This is a caricature obviously untrue, but it's a caricature Republicans will have to work overtime to change. We have to emphasize the positive ideas so important to us. Although we fight counterproductive federal programs, we should enthusiastically support programs that help children and families without tearing them apart.

With that in mind, I took action early in 1984 to consolidate Republican ideas for strengthening the family and to formulate new strategies for federal programs to help America's children and their families. I have brought many of these positive, profamily approaches together in a series of bills called the Comprehensive Child and Family Act.

The bill covers financial help for families, care of the aged

4

and handicapped, help for the homemaker with young children, education, drug abuse, youth employment, adolescent pregnancy and sexual activity, pornography, child abuse, and family violence.

The bill treats family problems in family-oriented ways, not government-oriented ways, and embrace the principle that there is *absolutely no substitute for the family.*

The foundation of this legislation came from my work on a new committee of the House of Representatives, the Select Committee on Children, Youth, and Families. We have listened to days and days of testimony and read thousands of pages of findings and statistics. Despite horrific accounts of failed government efforts and their tragic effects on hundreds of thousands of American families, Democrats cling to the old ways, and are fearful of change.

Those old ways have failed. It's time for the Republican way.

Consider the critical dilemma of adolescent pregnancy. In 1982 there were nearly three-quarters of a million illegitimate births in the United States. Almost half of these were to teenagers. Young girls, still children themselves, were now responsible for the care, protection, and development of infants in need of special attention.

Since the 1950s the number of illegitimate births to teenagers has increased over 500 percent! That's a staggering increase when we realize that today 2.8 million children are living in households where the mother has never been married. Over 60,000 of these children live in my home state of Virginia.

Despite so-called modern attitudes about the family and child development, it's still true that children need love, care, and attention from mothers *and* fathers. In other words, families are still the basic foundation for a healthy and happy childhood. Even in situations where one of the parents is missing, single parents take great efforts to make things as normal as possible. *Normal* means *family*.

Today in this country, government programs are geared primarily to trying to help people *after* they've gotten into trouble. The priority is not prevention.

In other words, if a twelve- or thirteen- or fourteen-year-old girl has a baby, the government provides medical attention, services, and money—everything to make it easier to live with the consequences of her irresponsibility. There is relatively little attention given to preventing the pregnancy in the first place. This has got to change.

Let's face it, children that age are just too young to be engaging in sexual activity. It is morally and psychologically ridiculous to suggest otherwise. Liberals are quick to tell young people that it's wrong to take drugs, to shoplift, and to cheat in school. Why is it they're afraid to tell kids that it's wrong for them to start having sex? Is sex less morally significant than shoplifting? If people in government care anything about children, they must ensure that federal programs and officials discourage kids from making the wrong decisions. There is no way to remain neutral in situations like this.

The Bliley Comprehensive Child and Family Act, therefore, will help young teens postpone sexual activity. Professional counselors, educators, community workers, and, especially, parents will be encouraged to work together with children to help them see the positive social, personal, and moral advantages of saying no.

Right now federal programs attempt to stay morally neutral when it comes to this kind of counseling. But you can't pass out contraceptives, explain how all the different parts work, pat the kids on the back, and not expect them to feel encouraged to rev up their sexual engines. *Moral neutrality is a myth.*

6

Another feature of my legislation includes stronger adoption counseling for pregnant unmarried teens. Programs for pregnant teens which offer adoption as a realistic option have shown *adoption rates two to four times higher* than in agencies that don't stress all the possibilities. When adoption is chosen, life both for the young women and for their children is much better.

In addition, the government should *stress* that adoption of the baby is better than aborting a human life.

This combination of sensible moral advice, practical counseling, and realistic alternatives establishes a framework for young women to make responsible decisions by considering *all* the factors. Too often young women and teens make life-changing decisions based on the slimmest information.

Abortions, for instance, are chosen because it's the easy way out or there seems to be no other choice. Government programs advocate the quick fix, but the government should be the advocate for *life* and for the things that promote a *good* life.

This approach might seem obvious to some people, but it goes against the grain of current federal policy. In other words, commonsense approaches to problems are not the way of Washington's liberal establishment. But it's the commonsense approach that I've tried to take in my legislation and to apply to family problems.

For instance, my bill includes a homemakers' tax credit for families that sacrifice a second income in order for one parent to stay home and raise the children. Currently, only families choosing professional day care are eligible for assistance; that is, the government encourages *both* parents to get a job and leave their children with the pros.

If we're going to help children, let's be fair and help as many as we can. Some families might need help if they give up a second income to stay home with the kids. The federal government should be encouraging these parents to spend as much time as they can raising their own children. My profamily legislation also helps older Americans, not just the children. I want the Internal Revenue Service to give tax credits to families that care for elderly or disabled relatives at home. And medicaid benefits should be extended to cover disabled family members cared for in the home. These changes will allow families of limited income to care for their members at home if they can and remove government incentives to place older and disabled members in an institution.

As you can see, the kinds of changes I'm suggesting are designed to pull the family together and safeguard children. I'm hopeful that this legislation can be a way for all Republicans, and enlightened Democrats as well, to bring a more positive, commonsense approach to fundamental problems.

It's not enough to throw more money at a problem with the naive hope that only expensive solutions work. Neither is it enough merely to gripe and complain about the need to cut government spending. The children of America deserve and, most especially, *need* a lot better than that.

The government has a responsibility to tend to legitimate human needs. It also has a responsibility to implement some new and better ideas that don't create more problems than they solve. Republicans have the opportunity to take the leadership in this and show everybody their heartfelt, honest, and effective concern for our families and our children, both born and unborn.

And that means that there is a great deal that you can do to help me and to help the American family. First, *write your own congressman* and tell him that you support the Bliley Comprehensive Child and Family Act. Tell him to talk to me on the floor of the United States House of Representatives to find out what he can do to support this important legislation.

Second, make an appointment to *visit your member of Congress in his local office* to talk to him about my legislation and his views on the family. Take one or two friends with you (don't gang up on him) and *insist on talking personally with the congressman*. Politely, but firmly, decline any suggestions to talk with one of his aides.

You want to be able to look your representative in the eye and talk to him about one of the most important issues in our country today. If he refuses to meet with you, write your local newspapers and ask them if they know why your congressman refuses to meet with his constituents. That should get some results.

Third, *go to your congressman's next town-hall meeting.* Ask him in front of all the people there exactly where he stands on the Bliley profamily legislation. If he's for it, he deserves to have the praise of all the people in the room. If he's against it, he deserves to be embarrassed in front of a crowd. Let him try to explain why he thinks the liberal agenda has been such a smashing success.

Now this might not seem like much to do, but let me assure you that this kind of approach can work. If people all over the country demand a response from their elected representative, we're going to see some constructive action here in Washington: action that's long overdue.

Working together, we have the chance to do something good for America. The families of this country need more than political rhetoric; they need our help. And Republicans are showing the way.

The Cliché

"Democrats stick up for the 'little man,' while Republicans look out for big business, the rich, and the well-born."

The Republican party looks after the interests of big business, the rich, and the well-born. Its tax policies help people who don't need help, and its budget cuts hurt those who most need help. But Democratic policies help the "little man" and his family. Democratic politicians understand compassion; they help blacks, the poor, and those who need jobs and housing. Working-class Americans who want a fair shake should vote Democratic.

2

Who Helps the Little Guy?

By Philip M. Crane, MC

The above superstition, which echoes through the halls of Congress and throughout the land, had a germ of truth around the turn of the century.

As late as Al Smith's day, working Americans had in Smith a true friend. This was especially true of those new arrivals to our shores who found dignity in *any* work and who recognized that America offered countless opportunities to achieve goals denied them elsewhere.

Smith was the dominant influence in his party as late as 1932, when the Democrat platform committed the party to a gold-backed dollar, no tinkering with the currency, cuts in spending (it condemned the Hoover administration for the growth of bureaucracy), states' rights, and repeal of Prohibition.

Franklin D. Roosevelt not only ran on this platform, but solemnly pledged to *support* it, if elected, as no candidate had ever before supported a platform.

But contrary to their platform promises, FDR and the Democrats in Congress took us off the gold standard in 1934, and working Americans have been victims of the inflationary money policies of our government ever since. To make matters worse, those Americans in the lowest-income brackets—Americans who were not members of powerful unions and thus able to offset the ravages of inflation with major wage increases—were ground down to poverty levels during the heavy inflation of the Carter-Mondale Administration.

The human misery caused by the practitioners of "funny money" cannot be quantified. What we do know is that the tinkerers with the currency, the fine-tuners, have created a class of impoverished people out of what could and should have been hard-working, productive citizens enjoying the dignity of self-sufficiency and a faith in the future of their children.

Another Democrat, Grover Cleveland, probably understood the importance of honest money to wage earners better than any other U.S. president. "When the evils of unsound finance threaten us," Cleveland stated, "the wage earner—the first to be injured by a depreciated currency and the last to receive the benefit of its correction—is practically defenseless."

Even President Carter acknowledged that "inflation is the

11

cruelest tax of all." Yet, he could not persuade his big-spending Democrat-controlled Congress to help end it by reining in spending. If we refuse to be disciplined by balanced budgets, there are only two ways to deal with deficits: increasing taxes (directly or indirectly through inflation, which results from printing money to pay debts—that is, government counterfeiting) and borrowing.

Federal revenues today are at their highest peacetime levels, notwithstanding the Reagan tax cut of 1981. Since increasing taxes is always unpopular with politicians (and not sound economics in any event), the Democrat refusal to cooperate in reducing spending levels has left to the Treasury and the Federal Reserve System the responsibility of funding this red ink either through borrowing (and pushing interest rates back to the double-digit figures of the Carter years) or through inflating the currency.

The latter option not only will resurrect the double-digit inflation rates of the Carter years, but over time will also cause the bankers to add an inflation "fear factor" into what they charge for money, thus raising interest rates too.

As a result, the big-spending Democrats who control the House are sowing the seeds once more for double-digit inflation and double-digit interest rates.

How does this demonstrate compassion for the "little man"? Who in our society is going to feel the pain of this first and most severely? It's a cinch it won't be the "rich and the well-born."

It is not mere partisanship to pin this gloomy tail on the donkey. Since *all* taxing must, constitutionally, originate in the House and since all general appropriation bills originate in the House as well, it is important to recognize who is doing what to whom.

We are all aware of Tip O'Neill's expressions of alarm over "Reagan deficits," but the president has nothing to do with

12

spending. His function is to *execute* the spending policies *mandated* by Congress. The initiation of all general spending bills is an *exclusive* function of the House of Representatives, where Speaker O'Neill presides with a 100-vote majority.

Moreover, Democrats have controlled the House of Representatives for all of the past fifty-two years save four. And the last time Republicans controlled the House was thirty years ago! (Coincidentally, that was also the last time that Congress cut a presidential budget and that president was Dwight Eisenhower.)

If one needs further evidence of who's doing what to whom, he can consult the National Taxpayer Union (NTU) rating of members of Congress on spending. NTU makes no distinction between "good" spending and "bad" spending. It takes every vote involving the expenditure of taxpayer dollars, from welfare to weapons.

When one looks at the most fiscally responsible top fourth of the Congress (108 members), he will find only *five* Democrats. When one examines the biggest-spending bottom fourth of the Congress, he will find only *one* Republican among the big spenders!

The question then recurs: Who are the real friends of the "little man"?

Evidence of the need for truth-in-labeling by Democrat politicians can be found in their consistent opposition to indexation of the tax code, a bill I first introduced in the House in 1974. Indexing prevents individuals whose income has merely kept pace with inflation from being pushed into higher tax brackets.

Indexation was included in the Reagan tax cut in 1981, but no thanks to the liberal Democrat leadership in the House. The Democrat-controlled Ways and Means Committee would not even hold hearings on the measure. It

13

became law only because the Reagan tax package was constructed in the offices of Secretary of Treasury Don Regan and the offices of the Republican members of the Ways and Means Committee and the Senate Finance Committee—and because it won support from 48 "boll weevil" Democrats.

Since passage of the 1981 tax bill, Speaker O'Neill and the Democrat majority leader, Jim Wright, have said that Republicans passed a tax bill to benefit the rich at the expense of the poor. Moreover, the Democrats say indexation should be abolished before its implementation date in 1985.

But who benefits from indexation? Not the rich; they are already in the *highest tax bracket*.

Peter Grace, chairman of the much-esteemed Grace commission, which studied government waste, extravagance, and mismanagement, noted the impact since 1948 on today's $20,000 per year wage earner just as a result of failure to index the *personal exemption*.

This person's taxes over the past thirty-five years, in just this limited area, rose 135 percent. By contrast, the $100,000 wage earner today experienced only a 12-percent tax increase over the same period. And bear in mind that the *median* income today is $24,000.

Indexation of the tax code back in 1948 would have spared today's $100,000 wage earner his 12 percent tax increase since 1948 through inflation. But it would also have spared today's $20,000 wage earner his 135 percent tax increase.

Congressman William Thomas (R–Calif.) has noted, "Today, *one of three* taxpayers is taxed at 30 percent, as opposed to only *three out of a hundred* in 1969." If this were the result of real increases in disposable income, we could applaud it. However, it traces principally to the fact that today's dollar is worth only one-third of the 1969 dollar.

That is why Presidents Cleveland and Carter viewed inflation as such a cruel tax on low- and middle-income wage earners. But, inflation aside, these groups have *always* shouldered the lion's share of our tax burdens and always will. Government's appetite for spending is dependent upon the scores of millions of Americans in these brackets for its revenues.

Peter Grace stated, at Republican Study Committee hearings in September 1983, that if the government confiscated *all the taxable earnings* of those making $75,000 per year and above, it would cover the national government's expenditures for only *two weeks.*

So, who pays the taxes? The little man, of course; the person supposedly represented through the years by the Democrats. The same Democrats who are out to kill indexation. The same Democrats who have controlled the House of Representatives for thirty consecutive years. Even majority leader Jim Wright has not always been able to peddle his "friend of the little man" line with a straight face in floor debates.

Nevertheless, our Democrat friends are quick to argue that they are still the friends of the little man, for they created such departments as Housing and Urban Development to provide for the homeless.

One of the most squalid tenements in America is the Mott Haven housing project in the Bronx. Walter Williams, economics professor of George Mason University, has described Mott Haven as "one of the urban holes from which there is little or no escape for anyone unfortunate enough to fall in." Even presidential candidate Carter said in 1976 that this abominable hellhole needed change, and President

Reagan four years later deplored the fact that nothing had been done.

By the end of 1981, eleven years after HUD took over the project, the taxpayers had invested $22,000 per unit in a project that originally had 345 units. When HUD took over the project, the median price of a house in America was $26,000. At the end of 1981, all the units at Mott Haven were boarded up except for 105, and of these only 53 were occupied.

"Who has lost in the $8,300,236 tragedy?" Professor Williams asks. Not the banks and investors, who were paid off by HUD. "The losers," he concludes, "are the tenants, who thought they would receive better housing, and, of course, that good guy we all know—the taxpayer."

Williams notes, "The total number of housing units destroyed by urban renewal programs greatly exceeds the total amount of *all* housing created by *all* government housing programs. Taking only the years 1967–1971, 538,000 units were demolished while only 201,000 were replaced. Furthermore, only 100,000 of the units replaced were for low- and moderate-income families."

John P. Roche, a former chairman of the left-wing Americans for Democratic Action, accused President Kennedy, with his urban renewal programs, of "replacing Negroes with trees." Father Theodore Hesburgh, president of the University of Notre Dame and a member of the Civil Rights Commission, in the 1970s, said:

These enormous federal programs . . . are coming in, supposedly to help the community. They want to rebuild our society. What has happened in many cases is that people who are presently in the worst situation have their houses swept out from under them by bulldozers, they are given very little help in finding houses, and they generally do worse than where they came from. This is immoral.

But we all know the Democrats are the friends of the little man!

Professor Williams has noted that if every dollar appropriated to help the poor were given directly to the individuals in need, the average family of four would receive an annual cash income of approximately $34,000. In reality, each family is receiving closer to $8,000. What happened to the remaining $26,000? It was siphoned off in the administration of these programs by what Williams has referred to as the "poverty pimps," the vocal lobby behind the poverty programs designed to "help the poor."

Friends of the little man! Talk to the little man for a second opinion.

The liberal Democrats are all heart and no head. Their concern for the poor is admirable, but their programs neither solve problems nor reflect compassion. And the ballooning deficits that accompany their conviction that throwing money at the problems will create utopia end up destroying the poor *and* the middle class. They destroy pensions, insurance policies, wages, incomes, and savings.

In the 1960s we declared a noble war on poverty. Numberless programs were begun, all with great fanfare and greater expectations. The poor in America at last had reason for hope. The New Frontier/Great Society Democrats had discovered and addressed their plight.

America was confronted in 1964 with a national disgrace—36.1 million of our citizens eked out an existence below the "poverty line." Program after program went into effect in the 1960s and '70s: food stamps, housing, medical care, transportation, day care, fuel subsidies, education, school lunches, and so forth. The list of programs seemed endless, but no effort and no cost were to be spared.

It has proven costly. In fact, the best estimates indicate that American taxpayers shelled out roughly $1.639 trillion

17

to end poverty between 1963 and 1983. And what was the result? The number of Americans below the "poverty line" declined over that time by only 1.7 million!

One can determine what the government's solicitude has wrought by dividing 1.7 million Americans into $1.639 trillion. By my calculations, that works out to $960,000 of taxpayer money to get each individual off the poverty rolls. At that rate it will cost the taxpayers approximately $330 trillion to remove the remaining 34.4 million Americans who are still in poverty.

To put trillions into perspective, suppose you started at the time of Christ a business that lost $1 million a day, seven days a week, from then until now. It would still take you 700 years more to lose your first $1 trillion!

If this is war, as waged by our compassionate humanitarian Democrat friends of the little man, any protraction of the conflict will guarantee poverty for *all* Americans.

Our Democrat friends would profit from studying history. Our Founding Fathers recognized, as a self-evident truth, that government does nothing well. Thomas Jefferson probably stated the case best when he wrote: "If we can prevent government from wasting the labors of the people under the pretense of taking care of them, they must become happy."

Jefferson also stated, "The principle of spending money to be paid by posterity, under the name of funding, is but swindling futurity on a large scale."

What is even more perverse is the Democrats' attempt to identify Republicans as the defenders of big business, the rich, and the well-born.

It was Democrat-controlled Congresses that pushed through the legislation to bail out Penn Central, Lockheed, and Chrysler, and most recently the biggest commercial banks in the country by pumping $8.4 billion more into the International Monetary Fund.

All the while, the liberal Democrats mouthed their concern for the little man. But thousands of small businesses were going bankrupt at the same time these liberal Democrats rushed to rescue the big corporations and banks.

Justice Brandeis warned us years ago,

Experience should teach us to be most on our guard to protect liberty when the government's purposes are beneficent. Men born to freedom are naturally alert to repel invasion of their liberty by evil-minded rulers. The greatest dangers to liberty lurk in insidious encroachment by men of zeal, well-meaning, but without understanding.

Examples of liberal, Orwellian "newspeak" could fill a huge book, and space does not permit further elaboration here. As to the cliché of liberalism that Democrats are the friend of the little man, we can find instruction in an exchange between Humpty Dumpty and Alice in Lewis Carroll's delightful children's book, *Alice in Wonderland:*

"When I use a word," Humpty Dumpty said, in rather a scornful tone, "it means just what I choose it to mean—neither more nor less."

"The question is," said Alice, "whether you *can* make words mean so many different things."

"The question is," said Humpty Dumpty, "which is to be the master—that's all."

We cannot permit the Humpty Dumpty Democrats to turn words upside down in the dialogue of this election year. If we succeed in preventing that in 1984, George Orwell can rest in peace.

The Cliché

*"All Republicans are country-club-
bers and fat cats."*

The GOP is dominated by fat cats and people who like to
attend the country club. Republican politicians have well-to-
do backgrounds, whereas Democrat officials have more
middle-class roots. The national Republican organizations
have so much campaign money because the party's policies
help the rich. A party must understand the middle class if it's
to govern fairly. Republican backgrounds and attitudes are
too elitist to pass that test.

3

Which Is the Fat-Cat Party?

By Bob Livingston, MC

The argument that all Republicans are fat cats is as old as
the Democratic party. But time lends the cliché no more
credence than it did the long-held belief that the earth is flat.

Republicans and Democrats are not separated by any
arbitrary standards of family income, education, up-
bringing, or professional status. They are separated by ideas
and philosophies—by beliefs of what our government
should be, and by visions of what our nation can and should
become.

Traditional Democrats—and we must distinguish

between national Democrats and the much more conservative Democrats from the South—tend to believe that government can and should provide the answer to every problem.

If a mother is poor, the government should provide her with money. If a father is unemployed, the government should give him a job. If an industry is weak, the government should subsidize it and throw up trade barriers to protect it.

Republicans, on the other hand, tend to view the role of government as being more limited, though not necessarily less active.

Yes, the poor mother and the unemployed worker and all the underprivileged should be provided with at least temporary government assistance. But, more important, they should have an economic environment that gives them the opportunity to advance through their own efforts and devices.

Instead of just giving fish to the needy, they should be taught how and given an opportunity to catch their own fish. To Republicans, the opportunity to help people provide for themselves over the long haul is much more important than the provision of short-term benefits, which too often leads to dependency.

Democrats tend not to trust the mysterious yet always rational decisions of the free marketplace—they want to tinker, target, and tax our way to some well-intentioned but unusually unreachable goal. Republicans, in contrast, tend to believe that government can best help the free market continue creating jobs by minimizing government interference.

The Democratic vision of the future is a government that can reach out to right every wrong, eliminate every need. Much more realistically, Republicans envision an America in full bloom; an economy constantly growing to provide more and better jobs; a nation where everyone has a chance to succeed, and where neighbors reach out to help neighbors

Those bipolar worldviews encapsulate the *real* differences between the two parties. Nonetheless, it has been convenient for Democrats to say that the difference in party affiliation derives, not from the depths of one's convictions, but from the depths of one's pockets.

Let's look at the facts, on *their* terms.

First, the more visible symbols of both parties: the U.S. representatives and senators elected to serve in Congress. If the GOP is the party of the fat cats, it would stand to reason that Republicans in Congress would be much richer than Democrats in Congress.

A study of the financial-disclosure statements of all senators and congressmen indicates that, on average, they are all reasonably well set financially. But the figures point out that the average congressional Democrat has more income and more wealth than the average congressional Republican.

In 1982 the average outside income—in addition to the congressional salary of $60,662.50—was $39,694 for Democrats in Congress and $31,946 for Republicans.

The average minimum level of asset holdings (the financial-disclosure statements list holdings only in categories—that is, $5,001–15,000, more than $100,000, etc.) for Democrats was $256,645. The assets of each Republican member of Congress were $8,000 less—$248,880.

The differences in those numbers are not that vast, but they are significant: the "fat-cat" Republicans in Congress, the highest officials of our party, not only are *not* vastly more wealthy than the Democrats, but are *less* well off.

The fallacy of the fat-cat argument is even more striking when we look at contributions to the two major parties.

Following the logic that the GOP is the party of American fat cats, we would expect to find Republicans receiving vastly larger contributions than those given to the Democrats.

The facts indicate just the opposite: in 1983, the average dollar amount of contributions to the Republican National Committee (RNC) was just over $27. But the average donation to the Democratic National Committee (DNC) *was around $500*. (It has been understandably difficult for this Republican congressman to get an exact figure or straight answer from the DNC.)

The RNC has indeed raised much more money than the DNC, but this is a reflection more of technique than of contributor demographics. Early in the 1970s, the RNC mastered the sophisticated methods of soliciting thousands of small contributions from the huge U.S. middle class through direct mail and phone banks. The DNC is only beginning to learn such direct-mail technology and has continued to rely on the relatively few, but very large, donations from select wealthy families.

Nor does the fat-cat argument hold for contributors to individual Democratic or Republican officeholders. Probably the most active group of fundraisers among members of Congress at this time are the thirty U.S. senators up for reelection in November 1984.

As of June 30, 1983, the thirteen Democratic senators running in 1984 had campaign warchests averaging $405,579. At the same time, the seventeen Republican senators running had an average of only $262,913 cash on hand.

And nowhere else is the Democratic ability to raise big bucks more apparent than in my home state of Louisiana. We held a governor's race in 1983. The incumbent

Republican governor was beaten by Edwin Edwards, a flamboyant Cajun Democrat who held the governor's mansion throughout most of the seventies.

Governor Edwards spent almost as much ($13 million) winning this most recent governor's election as President Thomas Jefferson did for the entire Louisiana purchase (which was transacted in 1803 for $15 million). The Edwards campaign ended up with a debt of roughly $4.6 million.

Now, it's part of the lore of Louisiana that we take our politics seriously, but Edwards' next move shattered even *our* standards of fundraising flair. He claimed he could have easily paid off the $4.6 million debt by getting together some of his fellow Democrats and hitting them up for $200,000 or so apiece. But instead he came up with a "better idea."

He would round up a few *hundred* of his "friends," collect $10,000 from each of them, and take them all to Paris for a victory march down the Champs Élysées.

In January 1984 Governor-elect Edwards chartered two jets, loaded them with over 600 contributors of $10,000, paraded the folk through the streets of Paris, took them to dinner at Versailles and to the gambling tables of Monaco, and *paid off his entire campaign debt*.

Now that's fat-cat politics at its best! In fact, at a net of over $5 million, it's probably a world record. But it wasn't a *Republican* fat-cat event.

These examples alone refute the cliché that "Republicans are fat cats." But consider further the demographic evidence. According to the Bureau of the Census, only 7.2 percent of American households in 1981 had incomes of $50,000 or more—the low end of almost anyone's definition of a fat cat.

But Republican party affiliation amounts to 25 percent of all registered voters, and about half of the 30 percent of the electorate calling itself "independent" tends to vote for Republican presidential candidates.

That's a base of 40 percent, and in most recent national elections, this figure of course runs much higher.

A Congressional Research Service study found roughly 40 percent of the middle class identifying with the GOP in 1976, 1978, and 1980, and an additional 11 to 13 percent calling themselves independent.

In 1976, 53 percent of the clerical workers and 41 percent of the blue-collar workers voted for Gerald Ford. In 1980, 46 percent of all blue-collar workers voted for Ronald Reagan. The polls indicate he began 1984 with about the same level of blue-collar support. Identification with Republican values goes way beyond any concept of "fat cats."

The Republican party is not a country club for American fat cats. The party appeals to the broadest base of the American middle class.

Nowhere has the broad appeal of Republicanism emerged more clearly than in Michigan in 1983 and early 1984.

After promising not to raise taxes throughout his 1982 election campaign, Michigan's Democrat governor James Blanchard proposed as his first move in office a 38 percent hike in the state income tax. The Democrat-run state senate quickly approved the tax increase, and the Democrat senators who voted for it ran into a wall of voter fury.

Incensed by the new taxes coming at a time when the area was suffering from almost 20 percent unemployment, blue-collar auto workers from suburban Detorit launched an effort to recall their tax-hiking Democrat legislators.

Members of the United Auto Workers circulated recall petitions, garnered enough signatures to force a recall election against two Detroit-area senators, organized and financed a campaign, and threw their senators out of office.

In early 1984, Republicans were overwhelmingly elected to fill the senate seats in the two heavily blue-collar districts.

The fervor in Michigan is representative of feelings

throughout the country. Average people don't want more taxes; they want lower tax burdens. They want a government that effectively provides essential services, but not a government that spends itself out of control. They want to work and prosper in a growing economy, not live on handouts from limousine liberals talking compassion while they run an administration that strangles the economy.

Those are the values of our people, and those are the beliefs of the Republican party. The matchup of those values and those beliefs shows why being a Republican has nothing to do with being a fat cat.

The Cliché

"Big tax cuts and high defense spending caused these huge deficits."

Ronald Reagan and his congressional allies are to blame for $200 billion budget deficits. First, they doubled the defense budget increases planned by President Carter. Second, their 1981 tax bill cost the federal government hundreds of billions of dollars. If Jimmy Carter had been reelected, this wouldn't have happened. In fact, his last budget projected a fiscal 1983 deficit of only $8 billion. Under Reagan, that year's deficit was $197 billion, over twenty-five times worse.

4

Who's Responsible for the Deficits?

By Hal Daub, MC

The federal government's two most important jobs are providing security from foreign aggression and encouraging economic health. Put simply: safety, jobs, and stable prices. The success or failure of any government rests on its results in those areas.

Ironically, people have criticized the Reagan administration and its congressional supporters *because* it sought to build our defenses and have stable prices with economic growth. These critics say increases in defense spending plus lower marginal income-tax rates for individuals cause deficits of $100 billion to $200 billion.

At first glance, tying higher defense spending and lowe tax rates to deficits might make sense. But a closer loo shows the relationship is not so neat, and that changes i defense spending and taxes would not work to balance th budget.

After President Reagan and congressional conservative passed the Economic Recovery Tax Act in July 1981, th nonpartisan Congressional Budget Office (CBO) sti projected a rise in federal revenues from $605 billion in 198 to $923.3 billion in 1986.

That's an increase of almost 10 percent a year for fiv years, even after we passed what was called "the largest ta cut in history." (Revenues can go up even as *some* tax rat go down because of the complex ways population growtl spending programs, and past tax laws interact with tl economy.)

In any event, that 1981 tax bill was supposed to giv Americans $1.138 trillion in tax relief over the followir eight years. If it wouldn't actually *shrink* the federal tax tak it would at least make the burden much more bearable tha it otherwise would be.

However, the 1981 tax cut was partially undone. In 198 the Congress passed, and the president signed, the so-calle Tax Equity and Fiscal Responsibility Act. It offset $28 billion of the tax relief in the 1981 bill.

In addition, higher social-security taxes raised the ta burden on working Americans by $270 billion. The Surfa Transportation Act of 1982 added a five-cent per gallon ta on gasoline; that plus other excise and user taxes amount to $21 billion in new taxes.

Finally, inflation-inspired "bracket creep" will add $4

billion more to the American taxpayers' burden during the 1980s.

What is left of the "big" 1981 tax cut is $77 billion, and that is *over eight years*. That means that no more than 5 percent of the deficit could be covered by completely rescinding the 1981 act—the remaining 95 percent consists of higher spending. The idea that American taxpayers should be punished for a deficit problem caused by higher spending is plainly wrong.

What's more, tax increases are inflationary. They rob the worker of spending power, and they result in higher prices for all goods and services affected. They cause deficits not to shrink, but to grow.

The argument that increasing taxes is the way to fight deficits was best addressed by Nobel laureate Milton Friedman: "You cannot reduce the deficit by raising taxes. Increasing taxes only results in more spending. . . . Political rule number one is: Government spends what government receives plus as much as it can get away with."

My own observations in Congress confirm Dr. Friedman's observation. In 1982 the Congress and his own staff forced a three-year $100 billion tax increase on President Reagan. Some conservatives backed it (I didn't). Our understanding was, we would get $3 in spending reductions for every $1 in new taxes.

In the end, that $3 in spending cuts turned into 11¢.

If the budget were balanced on the backs of the American taxpayer—as Walter Mondale and other liberals think it should be—just how much in the way of new taxes would be needed?

Well, the average family of four making $24,000 a year pays $2,218, or 9.2 percent of its income, in taxes. To keep up with federal spending, that would have to go to 16 percent of its income, or $3,832. That would be an increase of almost 73 percent—over $400 more in taxes for *each person* in that typical four-person American family.

Since 1958, personal income-tax revenues have risen by a factor of 8.31 (bad enough), while expenditures have grown by a factor of 9.25 (even worse). Obviously, that difference means a growing gap between outgo and income. But look more closely.

During those same twenty-six years that spending grew by a factor of 9.25, the defense portion of the budget rose by a factor of 4.9, but transfer payments (social security, medicare, medicaid, welfare, food stamps) *increased by 19.34 times.*

In other words, social-welfare payments have grown more than *three times as fast* as defense.

As a share of the federal budget, defense was almost 50 percent twenty years ago when John F. Kennedy was president; social-welfare spending was 25 percent. Today, under President Reagan, those numbers are nearly reversed: defense is 28 percent of the budget in 1984 and social spending 52 percent.

National defense is expensive, but don't forget that, whereas other spending is often undertaken by the states, national security is uniquely the duty of the national government. If it doesn't take care of national security, no one else will.

True, America spends more on defense in 1984 than in 1980. But our military strength hit a post–Pearl Harbor low under Jimmy Carter, and Ronald Reagan was elected on a promise to fix things. There are increases from year to year in almost *all* areas of the budget, but we should look at them in context to see if one item is growing much faster than others.

If defense spending has increased at a pace below that of

other outlays and tax receipts, and if total tax revenues have grown and continue to grow each year, then what's causing those big deficits?

A sick economy was responsible for *part* of our recent deficits. High interest rates, energy costs, and disincentives for investment and productivity sapped America's economic growth during 1979-82.

As our economy faltered, tax receipts were held down as unemployment got worse; an absence of business profits limited tax revenues flowing into the Treasury's coffers. During the long recession, government spending for unemployment insurance, food stamps, and welfare went way up.

But things turned around in 1983. Inflation was below 4 percent and looks to stay manageable for some time. The U.S. economy blasted its way out of four years in the doldrums. Essential to that turnaround were the incentives to invest and save contained in the 1981 tax act. Business and industry were able to generate profits that allowed for expansion and new jobs without having to borrow the money.

There's also good news if you look at the states. Not more than a year ago California faced huge deficits, rising costs, and declining tax revenues. However, less than eighteen months after the recovery began, California not only eliminated deficits but had a *surplus* of over a billion dollars.

George Deukmejian was elected governor on a pledge not to raise taxes. Even before he was sworn in, politicians and special interests were telling him California's *only* choice was to raise taxes. Instead the new governor made a commitment to lean budgeting that, along with a strong economic recovery, turned deficit into surplus almost overnight.

Had Governor Deukmejian enjoyed the media attention of his predecessor, he would now be touted as presidential timber. George Deukmejian worked the budget miracle everyone thought impossible.

Duplicating the turnaround on a national scale is not impossible, but it will require new policies and new attitudes. An advantage that the governors of California and forty-five other states have is line-item veto power. *If President Reagan had it, we'd be much better off*.

When the legislature in California sends a spending bill to the governor, he has the option of vetoing specific *parts* of the bill without having to send the *entire* measure back to the legislature. Not only can the governor single out expenditures for trimming but the legislature is much more careful in the first place, knowing wasteful items can be cut with the stroke of a pen.

An American president can veto a specific expenditure only if he is willing to *veto the entire bill*. This means a president is held hostage by a large spending bill.

For example, the Defense Department has long wanted to close military bases no longer needed. Unfortunately, powerful members of Congress have been able to keep these bases alive, costing hundreds of millions of dollars annually. Presidents have felt it easier to go along than to veto the entire defense bill.

(Remember when Jimmy Carter, as a brand new president, targeted a number of expensive, and unnecessary, water projects in an effort to reduce spending? He lost the battle—it taught him to forget the pork barrel when seeking to stop the federal budget from exploding.)

Comparing the budget process of the states with that of the national government convinces me that what's good for one ought to be at least *tried* by the other, particularly when the states turn deficits to surpluses and the government in Washington turns a bad deficit into a much worse one.

Most of the opposition to a line-item veto for the president comes from congressmen who like a system that lets them appropriate funds in a sloppy fashion. If an expenditure cannot stand on its own, then it ought not to be added to a budget already financed with borrowed money.

The answers to the federal deficit are not easy. They won't be found as long as the dialogue is cluttered with charges that we Americans don't pay enough taxes or that too much is spent defending our country.

The federal government keeps living beyond its means. It's not because defense spending is out of control (even with the buildup its part of the budget is relatively small), and not because you aren't paying enough taxes (the federal tax burden is much higher than it was six, twelve, or twenty years ago).

It's because (1) programs and laws force money to be spent no matter how much revenue comes in, and (2) overspending causes or worsens the high interest rates and low productivity that hold back the economy and keep you or your neighbor out of work.

We launched a good recovery in 1983. Four million jobs were added last year, which cut future deficit estimates by over $50 billion. Economic growth is the best way to chop down deficits, but it's just not enough.

If we don't reform programs and change unwise laws, *we will lose this recovery,* and the country will be worse off than ever. We'll be facing about $400 billion annual deficits and a $2 trillion national debt.

The president can help break the deficit deadlock. If Congress gives him the line-item veto, that will help. If his advisers will show more courage and propose bold tax and spending reforms to Congress, that will help too.

But Congress itself, especially the chamber I serve in, has the most to do. For at least fifteen years before Ronald Reagan came to town, Congress had defense on a stern diet while setting up dozens of other spending programs. It allowed inflation to run wild, pushing you and me into higher tax brackets even though our *actual* buying power hardly moved, or moved down.

Americans looked at all that and, in 1980, voted for change. We got it. The president's policies have rebuilt the military, cut inflation, held down the overall tax burden, and started a recovery. That's good. In fact, it's more than most people thought Reagan could ever do. And I was proud to help as one U.S. representative.

The liberal argument that an adequate commitment to national security and a reduction in the growing tax burden caused our deficit problem is obviously false. We are paying plenty in taxes and facing up to our security needs responsibly. The liberal line that Americans should pay more taxes and spend less for defense is a dangerous one; wisely, President Reagan and other leaders have rejected it.

The Cliché

*"The Republican plan for defense is
to throw tax dollars at the Pentagon."*

The Republican view of military strategy is to give the generals everything they want and ask no questions. Real defense spending is way up under Reagan, and his allies in Congress do little to help the armed forces properly use all this new money and weaponry. America must match what it needs to do with the wherewithal to do it; that won't come by throwing money at the military in a knee-jerk manner.

5

What Kind of Defense Is Best?

By Jim Courter, MC

Introduction

The United States today faces military challenges around the globe. These challenges are more diverse than at any other time in our history as a nation. Some of these tests are immediate, and have elicited a direct military response from the U.S. Direct American involvement in Grenada and Lebanon highlights some of those challenges to our interests. Other challenges are latent, requiring a strong defense posture and flexible forces to prevent conflict.

For the United States to defend itself and help its allies, a blend of economic power, diplomacy, and military capabilities is required. Economic power and diplomacy lose their force if not backed by effective military capabilities. How can we ensure that the United States has the military strength necessary to deter conflict, making certain the cost of conflict outweighs any benefit to a potential aggressor? If *deterrence* fails (if an aggressor thinks he can profit from war), we must be capable of succeeding militarily, ending conflict on the lowest possible level, on terms favorable to the U.S.

How can we ensure that the right resources are devoted to our national defense, and that these resources are spent effectively? The efforts of military reformers have focused upon how to make certain the taxpayer's dollar is spent as effectively as possible.

The Military Reform Caucus, a bipartisan group of eighty senators and representatives, takes a fresh approach to defense issues. Members of the caucus include, among others, Senators Sam Nunn, Gary Hart, and Jeremiah Denton, and Congressmen Bill Whitehurst and Ken Kramer. Nancy Kassebaum chairs the caucus in the Senate.

Formed three years ago, the caucus concentrates on neither budget cuts nor increases. It attempts, rather, to move our defense debate away from quantity, to quality. It seeks to improve national security by developing a more effective defense.

Every year Congress debates how much to spend on defense. What is the right number? Any arbitrary number or percentage increase does not have intrinsic value. Let's move the debate away from our obsession with numbers to the forces and strategy we need. As military reformers have emphasized, "more isn't better, less isn't better; only better is better." The threat to American interests must be assessed;

36

then American forces and strategy must be built to address that threat.

The main threat and challenge to American interests come from the Soviet Union and its proxies. For the past twenty-five years, and particularly during the decade of détente (1971-79), the Soviet Union has engaged in a steady and sustained military buildup. During the 1970s the Soviet Union spent 40 to 50 percent more for defense than the United States. The West, lulled into a false sense of security by the promise of détente, allowed its forces to deteriorate.

The Soviet Union now has the power and reach to challenge our interests anywhere in the world. The Soviet Union now has a blue-water navy that routinely patrols the globe from bases astride major trade routes and choke points. Supported by Soviet military assistance, Cuba is projecting its power into Central America and Africa, destabilizing these regions. The Soviets invaded Afghanistan, and occupy it. And they have used the threat of military intervention to force a crackdown in Poland.

Even President Carter's defense secretary saw the historic lesson: "When we build, they build; when we stop building, they build."

American Vital Interests and Strategy: The Reality of a Changing World

Although our vital interests remain constant, the strategy and forces we need to preserve deterrence and protect our vital interests change. Some of those interests are: protecting the territorial integrity of the United States and defending the Western Hemisphere from aggression; keeping American commitments to NATO and Western Europe; protecting the world's shipping lanes; protecting the oilfields in the Middle East and the friendly countries there.

37

In the past we've argued the benefits of a "2½" or "1½" war strategy. Some have extolled the necessity of a 2½ war strategy, while others claimed that a 1½ war strategy is more realistic, given our resources. That is, should the U.S. be capable of fighting on *two* main fronts at the same time, while also having the capacity to fight a brushfire war in the third world? Or is having the forces to fight simultaneously on *one* main front and one brushfire enough?

Now that the dispute between those two war strategies has become old hat, we have strategists, in and out of the administration, arguing about "horizontal-escalation" strategy. All of these concepts are vague or ambiguous, and have only marginally guided the composition of our force structure.

The shape of a national, "grand" strategy will be dictated by executive and legislative decisions. This means that development of any grand strategy will always be piecemeal. In many ways, a comprehensive grand strategy won't be grand at all, because, as a well-known strategist has said, "the realm of grand strategy is for the most part *terra incognita*—still awaiting exploration, and understanding."

But the framework for such a strategy is the same for all nations. The first step for a more effective strategy in the 1980s—while recognizing the central importance of NATO—is to see events in areas outside the European NATO theater not in isolation, but in regional and global terms. And responses to isolated crises must be considered in the global equilibrium of power.

The situation that existed in Grenada, for example, must be viewed not solely in relation to the island itself, but also in the context of:

- how other nations would perceive U.S. impotence if the endangered American students had been taken hostage (another Iran) or if the U.S. had refused the appeal of

the Organization of Eastern Caribbean States to restore order in Grenada;
- Cuban power and influence in Central America and the Caribbean;
- U.S. influence in the region, and in the world;
- Soviet ability through its proxy, Cuba, to destabilize the region, and what effect this would have on future Soviet calculations (would the Soviets be emboldened or more cautious?);
- what effect all this would have on the global balance of power, as one measure of the U.S.–Soviet balance of forces and influence.

Lebanon provides another good example of strategic thinking. U.S. policy options must take into account:
- the importance of Lebanon in the Middle East equation;
- U.S. relations with other Arab nations, and U.S. credibility when it claims to support moderate Arab governments;
- the Palestinian problem;
- the danger of polarization in the region, enabling the Soviet Union to exploit opportunities;
- the impact of Soviet involvement in the region generally;
- what it all means for the balance of forces and influence in the region, and also globally.

This is not to say that the policy choices become self-evident when examined in this form. This form of policy analysis and scrutiny is not wholly neglected today in forming national security policy, but it deserves more attention.

Two Kinds of Warfare

Our military must decide the most effective way to fight. The stronger we are, the less chance anyone will test us—preserving the peace. We must choose between two different kinds of warfare: attrition and maneuver.

Attrition emphasizes wearing down the opponent's forces by overwhelming the opponent with superior and overwhelming firepower. Success in battle goes to the side with the most materiel and soldiers. The Union won the Civil War with firepower and attrition, overwhelming the Confederacy with more men and more guns, more supplies and more firepower. We used the same tactics when we rolled over the Germans in 1918 and the Axis powers in World War II.

But attrition warfare is badly outdated. A different style is needed—maneuver warfare. The object is to destroy the enemy's cohesion, and the *opposing commander's ability to think clearly*. This is done by creating dangerous situations that catch him off guard. Because you act and react more rapidly in those situations, the opposing commander loses his ability to cope with them, and he loses the battle.

John Boyd, a retired air force colonel who helped design the F-16 airplane, is well known for his historical analyses of warfare. He has developed a theory showing the real nature of combat. His OODA (observation-orientation-decision-action) loop theory shows the importance of a maneuver strategy. The actor begins by observing. The observations create a "snapshot" of his position in time and place, in relation to his opponent. The faster one side acts upon these fleeting snapshots, the more that side disorients the opposition with swift maneuvers.

The party that consistently moves faster through the OODA loop cycle will win. The party that is faster in the cycle alters the situation, throwing the slower party's decision out of sync. The slower party's actions become less relevant with each succeeding cycle. The will of the slower party is broken when he realizes his actions no longer work. Defeat follows, with the slower party in a state of panic or passive collapse.

As Clausewitz, a classic strategist who lived during the Napoleonic era, said, the object in war must be to break the opponent's will. *When the will is broken, victory results.* The kind of warfare that does this is maneuver.

A strategy of maneuver needs strong and innovative leadership. We need changes in military education and incentive systems to get such leaders. General Edward C. Myer, onetime army chief of staff, designed COHORT to enhance unit cohesion (how well a group of soldiers work together); it is a good change in the army personnel system.

We must institutionalize maneuver in operational strategy. The army's Field Manual 100-5 guides the army's operational strategy. It is encouraging that it has approved the doctrine of maneuver. But the doctrine can't be a guide only; it must also be used and institutionalized.

People First, Strategy and Tactics Second, Equipment Third

Military reformers hold that, historically, the most important factor in winning wars has been people; strategy and tactics come second; equipment third. People, and strategy and tactics ultimately have more importance for America's national security than equipment. The military reform movement will make sure they get the attention they deserve. The fundamental lesson of Lebanon and the Falklands was the vital role of people; training was crucial in those conflicts.

Since the challenges to U.S. interests can't be predicted, the U.S. needs highly flexible, light, mobile forces that can respond quickly to crises anywhere.

The president's approval of the army's plan to create a new light division in 1985 is welcome. This new Seventeenth Division should be smaller and more mobile than any other in the army. The army's goal is to have the capability to fly the division quickly to third-world regions like western Asia, to fight on tough terrain. Being able to respond rapidly to crises helps deter conflict and spike challenges to American interests.

The U.S. role in Grenada and the British success in the Falklands show the need to devote resources to such forces. The Military Reform Caucus has special forces high on its 1984 agenda. It is also looking at the state of our rapidly deployable forces, and the development of lighter army divisions.

Quantity vs. Quality Debate: A Straw Man

Many critics of military reform have argued that military reformers seek to replace good weapons with larger quantities of inferior weapons. Such a straw-man quantity vs. quality argument is misleading.

We do not oppose high technology. There are great benefits to the free world's technological skill; this superiority should be exploited to enhance U.S. forces. Sophisticated science and industrial technologies help America's economic strength. Science and technology also strengthen our nation's military capacity to deter war, or, if necessary, to win it. The Soviets view hi tech as the West's biggest trump—they figure it's a big part of our deterrent.

We must do more to keep our military technology out of Soviet hands. Congress, during the last session, considered

42

e Export Administration Act. That legislation, designed to otect American military-related technology, must be ghtened. The leakage of Western technology to the Eastern oc hurts America. Although Warsaw Pact forces are merically superior, their advantage is now offset by our vantage in weapons quality. But the Soviets are closing in our technological lead; the qualitative gap is narrowing. is increases the costs of deterrence for the West, and reatens NATO's security.

The Military Reform Caucus values technological genuity. But state-of-the-art technology must always be ared to the specific mission of a system. We oppose high chnology that might fail under battlefield conditions. We e concerned about the costly goldplating of many weapons stems. Often these technological add-ons to weapons stems cause delays, inflating weapons costs with only a nimal increase in battlefield effectiveness. These ndencies are all symptomatic of a bureaucratic ocurement system in which competition is lacking and a anager's success is often measured by how much money he s for his particular project.

Look at the army's Bradley fighting vehicle, originally ended to be a cannon-firing personnel carrier capable of rrying twelve men into battle. The program has had a enty-year life, during which its complexity raised the cost elvefold (over $1.8 million per vehicle) and cut its capacity six men.

Technology often becomes part of the force without being ted enough, interfering with the reliability of the system as vhole.

The Future: Change That Works

Preserving popular support for a strong defense need bipartisan effort. Congress and the Department of Defense must work together, for a military policy second to none Efficiency and competition must be increased, and wast eliminated.

The Military Reform Caucus tackles these issues directl We've scored a number of legislative victories recently tha will improve the process of defense acquisition, getting th most out of your defense tax dollar.

The caucus got Congress to create an *independent* offi of operational test and evaluation. Poor testing leads more than wasted money and ill-equipped forces—it mak the public think that Congress and the Pentagon are carele with the taxpayer's money and soft on military contractor

The new office will impose strict standards of operation testing. Independent reports on testing will be made Congress. The director of the office, to ensure impartialit will be appointed by the president, and report directly to th secretary of defense. Congress will have more confidence the programs that function well, and a greater capacity to s mistakes corrected before they cost you billions of dolla

The caucus has also supported, and helped pass, a b requiring warranties from the manufacturers of weapon We're also considering HR 4005, dubbed the creepin capitalism bill, which would make the Pentagon increase competitive bids by 5 percent a year until there competition for 70 percent of its buys. The bill is now befo the House and Senate Armed Services committees.

We hope your congressman will support this bill, design to increase competition in our defense establishment. there were *real* competition for every nut and bolt t Pentagon bought, our defense bill would not be nearly high as it is. Creeping capitalism would also improve the quality and reliability of weapons.

These measures shape the processes that define and build U.S. forces that can win on the battlefield. This is more effective than focusing solely on influencing a specific weapon choice or a doctrinal decision.

Military reform must keep on emphasizing changes in process and reform of organizational structures. The caucus must continue to improve the ways the Pentagon does business. Reforming the process of development and procurement of weapons systems, the formulation of strategy and doctrine and force planning, must continue.

The threat to American interests is real. Let's build the forces that will enhance deterrence and win on the battlefield, should conflict come.

For further information, read:
- *On Strategy*, by Col. Harry G. Summers, Jr.
- *National Defense*, by James Fallows.
- *Reforming the Military*, by Jeff Barlow (pamphlet from Heritage Foundation).

For more details on HR 4005, write to:
Congressman Jim Courter
325 Cannon House Office Building
Washington, D.C. 20515

The Cliché

"The Reagan policies in Central America are costly, warlike, and immoral."

President Reagan exaggerates Soviet and Cuban troublemaking in Central America. His invasion of Grenada was overkill; whatever happened on that tiny island was of no concern to us. Under Reagan, the U.S. supports governments (in Honduras, Guatemala, and El Salvador) or military insurrections (in and around Nicaragua) that are dictatorial and just as bad as the communists they oppose. To avoid another Vietnam, we should end our military involvement in Central America and let the people there handle their own affairs.

6

What About Central America?

By Dan Burton, MC

Central America isn't a very large part of the world, or even of the Western Hemisphere. It's only about 1,500 miles long, or about the same distance as a trip from Denver to Washington. Its seven nations—Belize, Guatemala, Honduras, El Salvador, Nicaragua, Costa Rica, and Panama—comprise less than 200,000 square miles. The entire region is smaller than the state of Texas.

A few years ago, most Americans couldn't name a single Central American nation, much less want to go there. But things have changed. Economic upheavals, revolution, and war have placed this impoverished region on page one. Still, most Americans don't see the region's importance to us.

How could such a small area most Americans know so little about be so important to the United States? Why is President Reagan committing such large amounts of military and economic assistance? Why are we involved at all? Are we getting ourselves involved in another Vietnam?

No, Central America is *not* another Vietnam. Yes, it is of *direct vital interest* to the United States. Consider:

- Central America is at our back door. As President Reagan told Congress on April 27, 1983, "El Salvador is nearer to Texas than Texas is to Massachusetts." San Antonio is as close to Washington, D.C., as to Managua, Nicaragua. In fact, it is a mere *1,700 miles up the Pan American highway from San Salvador* (El Salvador) *to San Antonio.*

- Two-thirds of all our foreign trade and petroleum pass through the Panama Canal. During a six-month period in 1942, Hitler's submarines sank more tonnage in the Caribbean basin—right off the coast of Central America—than in the entire Atlantic.

- As our imports from OPEC have decreased, those from Latin America and the Caribbean basin have risen. The share of U.S. imports of crude oil and refined products from Latin America and the Caribbean *increased from 16.6 to 37.8 percent between 1977 and 1983.*

History

It may surprise many to know that at one time during the nineteenth century Central America was a single nation: the United Provinces of Central America. But civil strife destroyed attempts to centralize government. Since the mid-

1800s Central America has become, in the words of the Kissinger commission, "small countries weak and vulnerable to outside forces and with reduced possibility for economic growth and diversification."

The crisis in Central America today didn't happen overnight. It is rooted in a history of poverty and colonialism, and in poor geography (earthquakes are frequent, and the land mountainous). Land-ownership and wealth are concentrated in very few hands, with the notable exception of Costa Rica. There is virtually no middle class in most of Central America. Nearly 60 percent of the population is in poverty. Corruption in government makes ABSCAM look like a Sunday-school picnic.

From World War II until the late 1970s, Central America was actually on the upswing. There was growing demand for its products. Growth was substantial, and hope for a better quality of life growing.

The situation reversed suddenly. Imported oil costs shot up while commodity prices dropped. The governments responded by borrowing heavily. As interest rates rose, the cost of servicing that debt skyrocketed. Governments were forced to impose cutbacks in education, health, and other services.

A quality of life already poor grew worse. Conditions were ripe for revolution, and the Soviet Union and Cuba moved in to make trouble.

When the Sandinistas took control of Nicaragua in 1979, they received enormous support from within and outside the country, including the Carter-Mondale administration, because of their promises to replace a dictatorship with a democracy.

As with other Soviet-backed forces, their promises were nothing more than propaganda. President Reagan said it best: "The Sandinista revolution in Nicaragua turned out to be just another exchange of one autocratic rule for another, and the people still have no freedom, no democratic rights, and even more poverty. Even worse than its predecessor, it is helping Cuba and the Soviets to destabilize our hemisphere."

While the United States in 1979–80 was rushing economic aid to war-torn Nicaragua, the communist bloc was sending arms and military advisers. Today, those arms and advisers are in El Salvador and threaten peace-loving nations of Honduras, Costa Rica, and Guatemala.

U.S. and Soviet Influence

What has happened in Nicaragua since 1979 tells a lot about the character and motivations of both the United States and the Soviet Union.

When the Sandinistas took over, the economy was devastated. Some 40,000 were dead; many more were homeless. The U.S. provided nearly $15 million in emergency relief during the first ten weeks, including food, medical supplies, and housing assistance.

During the first eighteen months, the U.S. government authorized $118 million in economic aid—more than from any other developed nation.

We also actively supported *all* loans to Nicaragua from international banks. We helped them receive $262 million from the Inter-American Development Bank—twice what the Somoza regime received *in total between 1960 and 1979*.

What kind of aid was the Soviet Union providing? T-55 tanks, amphibious ferries, helicopters, and transport aircraft—all military. With the help of the Soviet Union and its friend Fidel Castro, Nicaragua militarized far beyond anything that country had ever experienced. It has secret police and more than 22,000 active-duty forces, trained by

Cubans and given Soviet-built arms. The Sandinistas have announced intentions to increase the armed forces to 250,000.

Once again, "good intentions" lost out to guns; the Sandinistas have now turned their sights toward Moscow, in spite of nearly $1.5 billion in economic aid provided by the West. Despite promises of *truly free* elections, freedom of the press, and other blessings we take for granted here in the United States, the Sandinistas have no plans, and probably never did, of allowing more liberties anytime soon.

The Soviet-Cuban next step, stirring up trouble in El Salvador, made clear their long-term strategy and its implications for the United States.

Ten days before President Reagan took office, the communist guerrillas in El Salvador launched a "final offensive" to take control of that nation. Fortunately, President Carter quickly responded by sending arms and ammunition. The offensive failed, but the drive by Soviet- and Cuban-backed rebels to conquer did not.

President Reagan reacted decisively and courageously in El Salvador by working to establish long-needed economic and political reforms and to give the government weapons to offset the infusion of Soviet supplies.

President Reagan's policy has always been straight-forward and responsible. It requires economic and human rights as a condition of economic aid. It addresses the need to combat outside influences by providing the El Salvadoran government with the weapons, ammunition, and training to defend itself.

President Reagan promised not to send American troops into Central America, and he's keeping that promise.

Has the government of El Salvador kept *its* promises? Yes. On March 28, 1982, free elections were held to elect leaders to a national assembly, an election the rebels were invited to take part in. They refused, threatening those citizens who voted. One woman, wounded and bleeding, refused treatment until she had voted.

For all the communists' terror, destruction, and threats of death, *over 80 percent of the people voted*. Despite destroying public buses, blocking highways, and attacking villages, towns, and voting places, the rebels could not stop one of the most remarkable displays of democracy in the history of the free world.

Not even in the United States, with elections free of terror, do we even come close to the participation of El Salvadorans in March 1982.

A two-stage presidential election was held in the spring of 1984. Commenting on the first part, the *Economist* of London observed:

"El Salvador's presidential election on March 25 was billed as the freest in the country's history. It probably was. Despite a monumental muddle which prevented many people from casting their compulsory votes, some 65-75 percent of the voters turned out to give their second slapdown to the 9,000 Marxist guerrillas [who] on election eve . . . blew up eight power pylons, plunging half the country into darkness. . . ."

What about the rest of Central America? Let's look at the two democratic governments: Costa Rica and Honduras.

Costa Rica has a long history of democratic government and the highest standard of living in Central America. It's so peaceful it doesn't even have an army.

In May 1982 Luis Alberto Monge was inaugurated as president. Because his government refused to allow the use of its territory for the supply of weapons to the region's communist guerrillas, Cuba and Nicaragua made Costa Rica a target for subversive activities. For example, Cubans and Sandinistas provided weapons and training for leftist

51

terrorists in Costa Rica. Nicaragua has instigated terrorist actions in Costa Rica, leading to increased tensions between the two countries.

A new democratic government was inaugurated in Honduras in January 1982. It has worked with the United States and neighbors in the region to neutralize the threat of the large military buildup in Nicaragua. Honduras successfully held free elections in March, 1984.

Cuba and Nicaragua promised to "spare Honduras" from the specter of revolution if it "remained neutral." Now both Cuba and Nicaragua are increasing their training and support of extreme leftist groups inside Honduras.

Honduras has sought to protect itself by maintaining the best air force in Central America. Its ground forces traditionally were trained to repel an invasion from El Salvador. The dramatic increase in the size of the Nicaraguan military, as well as the latter's increasingly sophisticated offensive weapons, has led Honduras to be concerned with the security of its southern border.

Although the nations of Belize and Panama have not experienced similar insurrections, they watch the United States to determine if we will abandon our efforts—and our friends—in Central America. The world is watching, waiting, to see if we've lost our will.

Castro's Motive

A clear pattern has developed in Central America. Fidel Castro, with full backing from the Soviet Union, wants control of a region vital to the interests of the United States.

He hasn't stopped with the nations of Central America. He had *hoped* to use Grenada too—a successful U.S. rescue mission to the small Caribbean nation proved that. Castro's control of Grenada would have given him a springboard to

Central America with easy access to the choke points of the Caribbean.

Grenada is just north of Trinidad, a major transshipment point for over half the oil imported into the U.S. With Castro in control, one of our most important lifelines would have been threatened.

A 10,000-foot runway being built at the Port Salines airport would have handled military supplies and reconnaissance flights by Soviet and Cuban aircraft. The communist leader Maurice Bishop said the runway was to help the nation's tourist trade. Yet there were no other tourism developments going on, and no efforts to promote tourism on Grenada.

How much of a threat could the runway have been? I'm reminded of a story President Reagan told about Libyan transport planes supposedly flying medical supplies to Nicaragua. They were forced to stop in Brazil for refueling.

When Brazilian authorities discovered military supplies aboard the planes, they were kept from taking off again. Had the airport at Port Salines been in operation, they could have landed, refueled, and delivered the supplies without delay.

While our mission in Grenada was designed to rescue American medical students threatened by a bloody coup, it reaped more than we bargained for. It denied communist revolutionaries another foothold in the Caribbean, and denied them an excellent refueling stop for aircraft flying from Africa.

And what has happened since? The United States is providing more than $100 million in economic aid and establishing joint trade efforts to develop this small nation. We are now helping a provisional government set up free, democratic elections as soon as possible—something no Soviet client state has ever done.

Did the President do the right thing by going into

Grenada? Did the students need to be rescued? Ask the students.

Students were seen kissing the ground after returning to the United States. Polls showed that Americans supported what the President did by an overwhelming margin.

A trip made by myself and three other congressmen—Mark Siljander (R-Mich.), Bob Davis (R-Mich.), and Don Ritter (R-Pa.)—and funded by the National Defense Council, gave us evidence the Soviets and Cubans had but one interest in Grenada: *exporting revolution and terrorism*.

The President and His Opponents

President Reagan's goals in Central America are: (1) improve the quality of life of all citizens through economic and political reforms; (2) combat armed militants supplied by Cuba and the Soviet Union, and enable freedom-loving Central American nations to defend *themselves*.

President Reagan agrees with most Americans—we have no business sending our troops into Central America. We will not become directly involved unless our national security is at stake.

So why are the president's opponents in Congress, particularly in the Democrat-controlled House, characterizing the Central America problem as "another Vietnam," when it clearly isn't? Why are they so vehemently objecting to our policies (particularly military aid) without a cross word for Castro or the Soviet Union?

The answer lies in one word: politics. The Democrats have always been eager to paint President Reagan as a warmonger, hoping to make political hay at the polls.

President Reagan could have fought fire with fire. He didn't. Instead, he rose above partisanship and appointed a bipartisan commission on Central America. Headed by

Henry Kissinger, former secretary of state, it included key Democrats like Lane Kirkland, AFL-CIO president; Henry Cisneros, mayor of San Antonio; and House Majority Leader Jim Wright.

"This is not a partisan issue," the president said. "It is a question of our meeting our moral responsibility to ourselves, our friends, and our posterity. It is a duty for all of us—the president, the Congress, and the people. We must perform it together. Who among us would wish to be responsible for failing to meet our shared obligation?"

And what happens if we fail in Central America? If past communist successes are any indication, there will be a massive influx of refugees—perhaps as many as ten to twelve million—into the United States.

Moreover, our interests and our security will be threatened. Our ability to respond to crises will be greatly diminished. We will lose respect in the world.

President Reagan is helping to thwart Castro's plans. He has *reduced* the possibility of more direct American involvement in the future by helping Central American nations overcome severe economic and political troubles.

The story of Central America is a sad one. But there is hope. President Reagan's policies are working. The region is still economically impoverished, but the seeds of democracy and economic reform have been sown, and eventually the quality of life for all Central Americans will improve.

Is this aid expensive? It certainly is. But an ounce of prevention now is worth a pound of cure.

The Cliché

"Republican budget cutting always leaves defense spending intact."

A Republican administration and its conservative friends in Congress go after everyone else's budget except the Pentagon's. They seem to believe that military spending can go up nearly 40 percent in Reagan's first three years with hardly any waste, fraud, or abuse. If the American military machine is to be cost-effective, and if our force structure is to be lean and mean, it probably will take a Democratic president to make it happen.

7

Defense: Is It a Sacred Cow?

By Bill Dannemeyer, MC

For the past two decades, ever since elitist liberals gained control of the Democratic party, most Democrats have pressed for greatly reduced defense spending. As a result, expenditures for national security declined in the Carter years to less than a quarter of the federal budget. By way of contrast, John F. Kennedy's defense spending ran to about half of his federal budget.

The savings achieved through lower defense spending were not passed along to taxpayers by Democratic congresses, however, but used to boost various social-welfare programs benefiting the special interests that form the constituency of the Democratic party.

Republicans have traditionally supported a strong national defense posture, no doubt out of the realization that America's security comes first: if this country were to be defeated or isolated, or our global markets and raw materials such as crude oil cut off, any concern about federal welfare programs or redistribution would be academic. National security *must* come first. The protection of our citizens is the foremost and gravest duty of the federal government.

Unfortunately, those who do support national security—both Republicans and conservative Democrats—have occasionally blinded themselves to the waste and folly that do exist in numerous military procurement programs run by the Pentagon. Cost-effectiveness ought to be—but often hasn't been—a key concern. Indeed, the higher the quality and durability and battle-effectiveness of our arms systems, the fewer of them we need. Quality can be cheaper than quantity.

The idea that more money automatically produces a stronger defense, and the idea that less defense spending puts us even further behind the increasingly menacing Soviets, deserve closer scrutiny. There is fat in the defense budget—and plenty of it. Unfortunately, much of it was built into the defense budget by Democratic congresses more interested in military pork-barrel spending on unneeded bases or antiquated shipyards than in providing the sinews of real national security. If the Pentagon were freed from the burden of all this congressionally mandated fat, it could produce a leaner, tougher army, navy, and air force with a lot less money.

What can be done? The liberal Democratic leadership barely even acknowledges the national defense crisis resulting from an unprecedented and massive Soviet arms buildup—a crisis heavily documented and well understood in all the world's capitals. These liberal Democratic leaders are simultaneously pushing for major reductions in defense spending, and resisting all efforts to rid the military of costly pork-barrel projects such as useless bases. In short, the Democratic leadership supports the fat, and refuses to fund the lean.

That suggests that the only real hope for a *lean, strong* military, sufficiently funded to keep America safe, rests with the Republicans and President Reagan. Only a Republican majority, able to set the agenda for the House of Representatives, can really ensure the twin objectives of economy and sufficiency will be met.

One way to achieve real savings is to pursue the recommendations of President Reagan's Private Sector Survey on Cost Control, commonly called the Grace commission. It was chaired by Democrat Peter Grace, and its report is the result of millions of dollars of *donated* corporate executive time and expertise. This bipartisan group of public-spirited citizens compiled an incredible 2,478 recommendations for reducing government costs without reducing government functions or services. In fact, some of their recommendations would allow the government to perform more services than it does now. What the Grace commission came up with was potential cost-cutting measures that could save $300 billion over the next three years. Many of these proposals deal with defense. All of the proposals deserve our attention and respect, coming as they do from a bipartisan group of concerned private citizens.

Specifically, the Grace reports suggest over the next three years that $92 billion could be saved from the defense budget without impairing America's military posture. Nearly all of these recommendations involve managerial or policy improvments; none involves the elimination of any vital weapons or services.

Four of these reports—Office of the Secretary of Defense, Air Force, Army, and Navy—contain most of the defense recommendations. Reviewing merely the big-ticket items will show we can indeed cut the defense budget fat without removing any muscle.

In the report on the air force, $1.1 billion can be saved by implementing accrual accounting methods, which recognize expenses at the time of consumption instead of at the time of order. Accrual accounting is used in the private sector and is, in fact, required by law to be used by the Defense Department. Actual implementation would save a lot of money.

Modernization of the air force's automated data-processing equipment would save nearly $600 million. Both hardware and software are presently obsolete and cumbersome. Replacing this equipment with new state-of-the-art technology would not only save money but also improve military capabilities.

The Service Contract Act was enacted in 1965 to ensure that prevailing wages are paid to all workers covered by such contracts. The air force had nearly 27,000 such contracts in fiscal year 1981 at a cost of $1.9 billion to taxpayers. This law is wasteful, burdensome, inflationary, and impossible to administer economically. It is not subject to review by the courts or the comptroller general, and has outlived its usefulness. Elimination would result in a three-year saving of $2.4 billion.

The Davis-Bacon Act, in force since 1931, is another law that has long outlived its usefulness. The act was intended to prevent cheap, itinerant labor from swamping urban areas hard hit by the depression. The reverse is now generally true; *highly paid urban workers prevent workers in lower-cost areas from obtaining government contracts.* This not only helps fuel inflation but also makes for unnecessary cost overruns in federal contracts. It also causes unemployment. Elimination of Davis-Bacon would save $1.3 billion.

The spare-parts breakout program was designed to allow spare parts to be obtained from *other than* prime contractors. Unfortunately, less than 25 percent of these parts are competitively procured. Modifying this program to allow potential suppliers greater access to technical data before the procurement process begins would save $700 million.

The Walsh-Healey Act of 1936 is another obsolete law. It sets prevailing wage rates for government contract employees in transactions over $10,000. Not only have protections afforded by this law been covered by later laws, such as the Fair Labor Standards Act, but today over 50 percent of air force procurement purchases exceed $10,000 apiece. Walsh-Healey needs to be amended or repealed to allow *flextime,* which is allowed in other federal departments and agencies. Flextime would allow constant productivity without having to pay overtime, increase competition, and reduce contractor expenses, thereby reducing the cost of those contracts.

Increased use of multiyear procurement would save $2.4 billion over three years. Contracting for fixed periods from one to five years, with a lower ceiling on cancellation costs, would help prevent excessive cost overruns and price hikes. And a multiyear budget would also greatly help in being able more accurately to project future costs.

Dual-sourcing is another way to save much money. Dividing production between two contractors allows greater quality control and should be implemented wherever feasible and cost-effective. Some $2.4 billion can be saved in this manner.

Contracting out (to private enterprise) should be accelerated; studies have shown that savings average 59 percent over "in-house" production. Except where internal security is an overriding consideration, where no satisfactory commercial source is available, or where the privately contracted cost would be higher, contracting out ought to be made the rule, not the exception. Savings over three years would net $300 million.

The army should use better management techniques in its acquisition of major weapons systems. Proper engineering and management of technical activities, quarterly status reports to minimize last-minute changes, separation of procurement from production, and other enhancements can result in savings of $2.6 billion. Lack of proper coordination is a real a problem. There are just too many loose ends that can be better controlled through a more centralized administration of production.

Procurement, always a cost-overrun nightmare, can be enhanced through adoption of a *biennial budget* with an accompanying audit trail. This will enable defense managers as well as Congress more accurately to project program costs and to correct errors with a minimum of loss. Savings would be $6.6 billion over three years.

Better management of army ammunition would produce savings of $300 million. The ammunition program, considered poor and inadequate since Vietnam, suffers from a disregard for production schedules, duplication of inventories, inefficiency, and waste. Establishment of an *ammunition working capital fund,* with a single manager responsible for inventory control and production schedules, would go a long way toward reforming this chronic headache.

Like the air force, the army could save large sums by updating its automated data-processing equipment. New, standardized software, state-of-the-art hardware, systems integration, unified command management, and long-range planning would produce a net saving of $800 million.

Cost containment is another area in which central coordination, accompanied by audit reviews, would result in sizable savings—in this case, $1.2 billion over three years.

At army bases, support services include civilian personnel, police, firemen, finance, maintenance, custodians, and utilities. These should be coordinated under a single manager, with a strict timetable, and with increased use of contracting out. A saving of $700 million could be realized this way.

Navy production rates and program stability presently suffer from unrealistic inflation projections. Technical difficulties are underestimated, program guidance is inconsistent, and there is a constant "requirement creep," meaning that these specifications continually change. Programs need to be restricted to those that can be funded at economical production rates, a reserve needs to be maintained to help eliminate cost overruns, and consistent centralized management with a two-year budget are required. Accordingly, $3 billion could be reduced from current spending.

Multiyear procurement is another area in which the navy could save money—nearly $800 million. Improved efficiency, lot-buying in quantity, decreased financing, better utilization of facilities, and reduced administrative burdens could yield a 10 to 20 percent saving in unit costs.

As is the case with the air force, dual-sourcing would reduce navy costs from 12 to 52 percent, conclude twelve different studies, varying according to program and system. Some $1 billion could be saved.

Updated automated data processing would, for the reasons applicable in the other services, both strengthen our military capacity and yield substantial savings, in this case $1.5 billion.

In the office of the secretary of defense, inventory management is hampered by high maintenance charges, obsolete equipment, limited capacity, and lack of timely data. These are all correctable by upgraded computerization and proper administrative controls. Such correction would save $3.2 billion.

Base realignments and closures always face rough going since congressmen don't like to cut anything in their home districts. However, there are 5,600 separate U.S. military installations with two million active personnel, one million reservists, one million civilian employees, one million retirees, and a multitude of dependents. The annual operating cost: $20 billion. Of these installations, 4,000 are in the United States, to the tune of $14 billion. And of these, only 312 are considered "significant"; the remainder are regarded as "support facilities." Many of these facilities could prudently be either reassigned or closed without hurting our national defense. And $2.7 billion would accordingly be cut from the defense budget.

A major stumbling block in trying to keep down defense costs has been MILSPECS—military specifications, those little requirements that prevent a bolt used in a navy plane from being used in an air force plane. The services need jointly to develop common parts and standards to avoid the high cost of verification and acquisition. Special MILSPECS ought to be retained only when necessary. A whopping $7.5 billion could come off the deficit.

New starts of major weapons systems need to be integrated with a timetable to prevent overextension and cost overruns. Wise management could save $1.5 billion.

Current instability in the weapons acquisition process arises from fragmented budgeting. The selection process, internal DOD budgeting, and congressional appropriations are not sufficiently tied together. Multiyear procurement and a five-year budget plan are necessary to set economical production rates as well as coordinate programs. Some $7.2 billion could be saved.

A centralized procurement audit service, reportable to the DOD inspector general, would eliminate many of the problems caused by lack of integration and coordination. There are *four* different audit services lacking overall jurisdiction. Better management could save $1.7 billion.

There are many more recommendations in the Grace commission report. Countless others have been offered through the years by the General Accounting Office, the Congressional Budget Office, various administrations, numerous congressional and business groups, and a host of other sources. But the Grace commission's findings are not only the most recent but also quite extensive in scope.

What, if anything, will be done to cut wasteful in defense spending remains to be seen. Final responsibility, as with other budget matters, rests with Congress, and especially the Democratic leadership in the House of Representatives. *Republicans are willing to cut the fat but not the muscle.* A task force appointed by a Republican president has produced a voluminous analysis on where and how it can be done. The $93 billion that could be saved would go a long way toward reducing our budget deficits over the next three years. But for all its rhetoric on the need to trim the defense budget, the Democrat majority in Congress would really rather strip us of our *muscle*—our necessary military capabilities. The liberal Democrats are not concerned about saving you, the taxpayers, any money.

The Cliché

"The Reagan tax cuts aren't helping middle-class Americans."

The 1981 Economic Recovery Tax Act did almost nothing for the typical working American and his family. Polls show that 75 percent of the people think federal taxes have stayed the same or increased under the Reagan administration. Most of the breaks in that 1981 bill went to corporations and the rich, leaving bigger deficits for the rest of us. People in the high brackets saved a lot of money, but those in the middle brackets got peanuts.

8

Who Are the Reagan Tax Cuts Helping?

By Richard T. Schulze, MC

With the support of the American people, and over the opposition of liberal members of Congress, President Reagan was able to pass the Economic Recovery Tax Act of 1981 (ERTA). This legislation put into place large tax reductions that helped all Americans.

Opponents of the tax cut assert that benefits went mainly to big business and the wealthy. Let's look at the record. The economy has made a strong recovery. The most recent figures show housing starts running at a level of almost two million units per year, up from 900,000 units in June 1982. The unemployment rate has dropped much more than even optimists felt possible. The January 1984 rate of 8.0 percent was down from the high of 10.8 percent at the end of 1982. By April 1984 unemployment had fallen to 7.8 percent.

The economic turnaround would not have been this strong without the action taken by the president and congressional Republicans to reduce taxes. Businesses and investors, large and small, corporate and noncorporate, had to have the money to plow back into productive enterprises to achieve real growth. Without this growth we still would have unemployment in double digits.

By the second quarter of 1983, real GNP had registered an extraordinary 9.7 percent growth rate on an annualized basis. This contrasts sharply with the 5.5 percent decline in real GNP growth during the first quarter 1982. Opponents of the tax cut ignore the fact that there is a time lag between the implementation of an economic policy and its benefits. Even so, the tax cuts, combined with the reduction in the rate of growth in federal spending, are doing the job they were intended to do.

Before ERTA, individual income-tax rates began at 14 percent and ranged up to 70 percent on so-called passive income (interest, dividends, rents, royalties). However, a maximum tax rate of 50 percent generally applied to personal-service income. This "earned" income included such items as wages, salaries, professional fees, and amounts received from pensions and annuities.

The 50 percent maximum tax rate applied to single individuals with taxable personal-service income above $41,500 and to married couples above $60,000. This was so because prior rates exceeded 50 percent at those levels.

ERTA provided for the reductions in individual income taxes by means of a three-year across-the-board cut in tax rates. With the final round of changes in withholding rates in July 1983, and with the tax-liability calculations projected for calendar year 1984, marginal rates and income-tax burdens will be about 23 percent less than they would have been under Carter-era law.

Immediately before ERTA, the average income-tax burden, as a percentage of income, was higher than any other time during the preceding two decades. This means that the pool of funds taxpayers could keep after paying their taxes was at its lowest level in twenty years. Individuals could not save or invest as much as they wanted, or buy the goods and services they needed.

ERTA reversed this damaging erosion of after-tax income in four ways:

1. For 1981, there was a credit of 1¼ percent of the tax due on April 15, 1982. This figures out to a 5 percent reduction in tax burden, but because the Congress delayed so long in passing the president's program, it was not possible to implement it until the withholding tables were issued effective October 1, 1981. In other words, the rates took a dive, but the change was for only part of the year.

2. For 1982, there were across-the-board rate reductions averaging about 10 percent below rates of prior law.

3. For 1983, there was another 10 percent reduction, resulting in rates about 19 percent below rates of prior law.*

4. Finally, for 1984, the permanent withholding and rate

---

* The two 10 percent reductions lead to a 19 percent, rather than a 20 percent, reduction because the second 10 percent is applied to the rates in effect after the first 10 percent reduction.

schedules went into effect, bringing the across-the-board reductions to approximately 23 percent below rates of prior law.

The tax reductions include beneficial provisions (such as a reduction in the marriage penalty tax) phased in over different time frames, reflecting different objectives.

Congress wanted to encourage significant increases in personal savings to create a reserve of funds to finance additional investment in plants and equipment. The after-tax yield on investment had to be improved and the attractiveness of nonproductive tax shelters reduced. (This was done by reducing the highest marginal rate by 20 percentage points on January 1, 1982, rather than phasing it in as was the case with other rate reductions.)

What all this means is that high-bracket taxpayers did receive a heavy reduction in the marginal tax rates early in the three-year phase-in period, but for taxpayers in the lower brackets there was a corresponding speed-up in rate reduction during the later years.

Comparison of the rate schedules before ERTA with those after show that couples with an earned income of $162,400 or more still continue at a 50 percent marginal rate even after all the rate reductions are phased in. The only major reduction from which they could possibly have benefited took effect in early 1982, but then only if they had significant amounts of passive income.

A couple earning $100,000 per year was receiving a rate reduction of 5 percent, from 50 to 45 percent, by 1984. A couple earning $20,000 per year was receiving a rate reduction of 6 percent, from 28 to 22 percent, by 1984. Thus, in aggregate reductions, the lower-income couple actually received a greater tax break than the higher-income couple.

It goes without saying that the total dollar reduction in

taxes is greater the higher the income level. But as to fairness, lower- and middle-income working Americans, who have always paid most of the taxes, received the greatest overall reduction in the tax burden.

ERTA also corrected a grossly unfair condition that faced American taxpayers. Tax indexing, scheduled to begin in 1985, will eliminate "bracket creep." During the 1970s, bracket creep became taxpayers' number one enemy. The taxpayer found himself on an accelerating tax treadmill which pushed him into higher and higher tax brackets formerly reserved for only the rich. Although only some 3 percent of taxpayers faced marginal tax rates of 30 percent or above in 1960, by 1981 bracket creep had pushed 34 percent of taxpaying America up to the 30 percent level or higher.

Sometimes we become so tangled up in tax talk we forget what the jargon means. Consider the word *marginal*. A marginal tax rate is the percentage you pay on your *last dollar earned.*

For example, if you worked throughout 1983 (let's say, as a babysitter) and made $3,000, you would not owe federal income taxes on the first $2,300 of that income—social-security taxes, yes; but not federal income tax.

However, you will owe 11 percent of $700, which came after the first $2,300, because you crossed from the "zero bracket" into the first income-tax bracket, in which you must pay taxes.

(That's how the progressive income-tax starts. For a single person, it goes all the way up to about $55,000, where you owe *50¢ of every new dollar you earn.* Two married individuals filing jointly reach the 50 percent marginal rate at $109,400.)

Now consider a truck driver who earned $35,000 over twelve months. The paycheck he brought home the last week of December determined what his highest, or marginal, bracket was for 1983.

If he made $2,300 during the winter, and stopped working on March 1, he would get back every cent of the federal income taxes withheld from his check (providing he didn't take another job and earn more money during the year).

Assuming he kept on working, our driver, in the last part of December, reached the 40 percent marginal rate as his salary passed $34,100. Therefore, he paid 40 percent in federal income tax on $900, which rounded out his 1983 earnings at $35,000.

So *marginal* rates are different from, and in many ways more important than, *average* rates. Average tax rates are found by dividing your twelve-month gross pay into your total tax burden for the year (after you received the refund).

Marginal rates are the tax bracket you achieved during the very last part of the year—sometimes even on the last day of the year.

Once you get above $2,300 and out of zero bracket territory, your *marginal* rate is always higher than your average income-tax rate. You keep paying more and more as you earn more and more.

The 1981 tax bill began the process of cutting those marginal tax rates by 25 percent across the board—for *all* workers, small businesses, and savers—to expand your incentive to invest, save, work overtime, or take a promotion.

The liberals say this was too big of a tax cut. I say, when a single person can still hit the 50 percent bracket—a bracket supposedly reserved for "the rich"—with $55,000 in earnings, then the tax cut was probably *too small*.

Under ERTA, about 80 percent of the relief generated by tax indexing will benefit taxpayers earning less than $50,000 per year. If Congress were to repeal indexing, which many political opponents (Mondale, for one) of the president want, the *tax liability of the lowest-income Americans would be increased in one year by ten times the percentage increase of the highest-income groups.*

Indexing provides a long needed tax break for the lower-income taxpayer. It introduces fairness into the tax system. Repeal of indexing would be disastrous.

In 1981 and 1982 the favorable benefits of the president's tax cuts were masked by previously passed increases in social-security taxes and the bracket creep associated with inflation's impact on a progressive tax rate structure.

Again, if you listen to the voices arguing against the president's program, they will tell you to look at your pay stubs to determine whether the 1981 law benefited you. If you look at *only* 1981, you will be disappointed. But if you compare the results in 1984 with what they would have been if the old law were still in effect, you'll be pleasantly surprised.

The 1981 tax law changes were designed to bring about economic recovery, just as the name of the act implies. The business tax law changes must be viewed in that light as well.

Businesses were permitted to reduce their taxes provided they made new investments in depreciable property, or invested in research and experimentation, or made other business decisions Congress favored. Business saved in taxes, and that is fine provided it has the effect of putting unemployed Americans back to work. And it has; *there were four million new jobs in 1983.*

Let's look at five reasons why the tax cuts benefit *all* Americans:

1. The tax cuts created jobs and will continue to encourage saving, and investment in new plants and equipment. More jobs in the economy benefit the lower-income taxpayers by getting them off welfare.

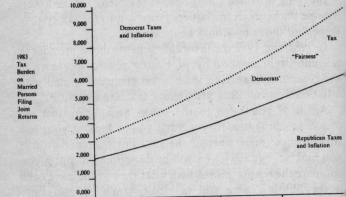

1983
Tax
Burden
on
Married
Persons
Filing
Joint
Returns

Democrat Taxes
and Inflation

Tax

"Fairness"

Democrats'

Republican Taxes
and Inflation

SOURCE: Internal Revenue Code of 1954; PL 97-43

NOTES: Republican taxes include the ERTA tax table and *adjust all
incomes for Reagan's average inflation of 3.85 percent during
1982-83.*

Democrat taxes include the pre-ERTA tax table and adjust all
incomes for 10.9 percent inflation for two years. *Carter policies
resulted in an average of 10.9% for 1978-81.*

Figure 1.

2. The tax cuts are especially helpful to small businesses because such enterprises are generally not incorporated and pay their taxes through the individual tax returns of their owners. Lower individual rates mean that small businesses will be more likely to survive and prosper, allowing them to provide most of the new jobs in our economy.

3. The tax cuts reduce the penalty for saving by removing the incentive for consumption. This means seed capital for new businesses and increased investment for established firms. Put simply, more business means greater employment.

4. The tax cuts have encouraged investment in taxable areas, while deemphasizing tax-exempt investments. High taxes had driven taxpayers at all income levels to shift their money from activities that benefit the economy to tax shelters that may or may not have economic benefits and encourage consumer spending. This leaves those who cannot afford such options to bear the burden of even higher taxes as the tax base is eroded. Who are those taxpayers? Why, the lower- and middle-income taxpayers, of course.

5. The 1981 bill counters bracket creep. Bracket creep is the cruel outcome of inflation interacting with progressive tax rates. It is also the mechanism by which a tax-and-spend government can raise taxes in real terms without passing a single law. The president's program is the first comprehensive effort to reverse the trend, and the major beneficiaries are average American taxpayers.

Finally, the critics of the tax cuts point to high deficits and high interest rates as undesirable results of reduced federal revenues. Their argument is that increased federal borrowing to pay for the deficits has driven interest rates up, drying up the source of new capital needed for personal borrowing as well as for business investment.

The truth is, the relationship between high deficits and high interest rates is complex and unclear. The prime rate stood at 15.75 percent in January 1982, when ERTA went into effect. The federal debt stood at slightly over $1 trillion. Two years later, in January 1984, the debt had risen 26 percent, but the interest rates had dropped to the current 11 percent range.

So let the doubters and critics beware. The tax cuts have been good for the national economy and for the American people, *rich and poor alike*. They have not been a sop to the moneyed elite. Instead, they have been the source of a remarkable economic recovery.

The president's program took time to go into effect, and thus far we have seen the results that were promised and predicted. My hope is for a continued reduction of the tax burden on the average American taxpayer by simplifying and, if necessary, modifying the complicated tax code.

If the efforts of President Reagan are allowed to progress and Congress makes a sincere effort to reduce federal spending, the mid-1980s will see economic growth and prosperity unequaled in the history of mankind.

The Cliché

"America should work for peace, disarmament, and human rights. Negotiation is always better than confrontation."

President Reagan made the world more dangerous by his increased military spending, threats to communist countries, and lack of sincerity at the bargaining table. No American likes the communist system, but we must deal in good faith with its leaders. A liberal president would work for peace and human rights, and put aside the warlike policies of the Reagan era. Let's hold back on our military buildup and cool the tough talk. Peace is too important to play games with.

9

Does Appeasement Ever Work?

By Floyd Spence, MC

It's often assumed that freedom is a consequence of peace. History is full of examples that disprove this, and yet many people continue to believe it. They seem to forget that peace without freedom is what people in jail have.

The only way to ensure continued freedom and peace is to see that the federal government performs its primary function: protecting our nation from foreign aggression.

This means eternal vigilance. Peace *and* freedom must b
guarded at all times.

The genius of the American system of government is th
belief that the central government should perform thos
functions the people, or political subdivisions, can't perforr
for themselves. Individuals, cities, and states can't b
themselves provide for their common defense. That's wh
the original thirteen states banded together to form thes
United States, and why the greater number of enumerate
powers granted to Congress in the Constitution deal wit
military matters in some form.

The primary duty of our federal government is to protec
us. That means fighting others who engage us in war. It als
means doing everything possible to *prevent* a war!

So the question arises as to the best way to prevent a wa

No country was ever forced into war because it was to
strong. The best way to prevent war is to stay so strong tha
no other country thinks it can win a fight against you. Bi
one sure way to invite attack and aggression is to send
signal to your adversaries that you are weak or indecisiv

The goal of a strong defense is to convince any adversar
that no advantage can be gained by threatening or beginnin
hostilities against you. True strength, and a perceive
willingness to use it if necessary, are the deterrents that kee
aggressors at bay. Peace is best achieved through strengtl

Twentieth-century events show how true this is. Fift
years ago in Europe people witnessed the rise of an ideolog
that threatened to conquer Europe and the world. Th
ideology was nazism. In the Pacific, a militaristic, imperia
Japan offered another, related ideology.

How did the world's free nations react to these clear an
present dangers? In February 1933, British students took th
Oxford Pledge, after the Oxford Union passed a motion tha

76

"this house will in no circumstances fight for its king and country." But the ironic part is that many of those who took that pledge ended up fighting and dying. Instead of promoting peace, as they thought they were doing, they were actually encouraging Adolf Hitler by sending him the wrong signal.

In 1938, the free nations of Europe once again offered Hitler a concession in hopes of buying peace. Prime Minister Neville Chamberlain returned from Munich proclaiming "peace in our time." The ink of the treaty was barely dry when Hitler moved to absorb all of Czechoslovakia in violation of the Munich agreement. The "peace" purchased at Munich only allowed Hitler more time to reinforce his position, while the free nations of Europe tried to make up for lost time and rebuild their defenses.

Europe was not the only area threatened by an aggressive ideology. Imperial Japan had begun its conquest of the Pacific in China even before Hitler had consolidated his position in Germany. But the United States continued to provide the Japanese with scrap metal and other materials for its war effort.

As if to signal our own indecision, Congress late in the summer of 1940 was able to muster approval of the draft by only one vote! And if this were not enough to confirm Japanese perceptions of American weakness, peace rallies were held up until December 6, 1941, urging the United States to seek peace with Germany and Japan.

World War II resulted not from "provocations" by the world's free nations (Great Britain, France, and the United States), but from Germany's and Japan's imperialist ambitions *combined with a judgment that the democracies did not have the will or the tools to fight.*

A weak and naive foreign policy is like feeding meat to a

crocodile: it's all right so long as you have enough meat, but when you run out, the crocodile will go for your arm, and eventually the rest of you, to satisfy its hunger.

After the devastating experience of World War II, the free nations faced a new and potentially more dangerous ideology: communism, as practiced and led by the Soviets.

At the end of World War II, the United States was the strongest military and economic power in the world. To give you an example of our resources, we had, at that time, a navy larger than the rest of the world's fleets combined. We were also the only country to possess the atomic bomb. We could have done with the world pretty much as we wanted and no one could have stopped us.

Instead of heeding the lesson of the war years in Europe and the Pacific, the United States in 1945–46 turned inward, disarmed, and sought to beat too many "swords into plowshares" in the hope that all other nations would follow our example.

Although we must always strive for peace and be willing to make concessions where there's realistic hope of progress toward this goal, we should also recall another, less well known biblical admonition:

"Proclaim this among the nations: Prepare war, wake up the mighty men. . . . Beat your plowshares into swords, and your pruning hooks into spears" (Joel 3:9–10).

As we read in Ecclesiastes 3, there is a time for all things. We must have the wisdom to know when and how to act in the best interests of ourselves and mankind.

For thirty years we suffered—sometimes mildly, sometimes severely—from guilt about being a strong and successful military and economic power. We tried to appease everyone, to buy our way through crises. America followed a policy of "preemptive concessions." We showed over and over that no matter what someone did to us, we wouldn't

78

ight back. We made unilateral concessions even in the absence of negotiations.

In 1977–78 we canceled the B-1 bomber and the neutron bomb unilaterally. We could have at least *attempted* to obtain concessions in return. But we didn't even try.

How could anyone expect the Soviet Union to negotiate seriously with us when we had a tendency to give in even before sitting down at the bargaining table?

A few years ago I met with Prime Minister Lee Kuan Yew of Singapore. He is our friend, but he said the United States didn't say what it means and it didn't mean what it says, as it once did. He pointed out that people in the world are choosing up sides between tyranny and freedom. *They want to think they're joining the winning side* and we weren't acting like a leader of the free world.

Instead of being a force for peace and freedom, we have tried to appease even our weakest adversaries. Many people have the notion that we will go to any extent to avoid an unpleasant situation, and if we are forced into a conflict we won't see it through a successful conclusion.

What will you get with such a policy? The Korean War, the loss of Cuba to Fidel Castro, the seizure of the USS *Pueblo,* and the Iran hostage crisis are a few of the answers.

The belief that we shouldn't hurt anyone's feelings, that we do not want to win wars, and that we will serve as the world's whipping boy was dramatically symbolized by that last helicopter leaving the American embassy in Saigon in April 1975. The photographs of people dropping everything and running, of people fighting for its landing gear as it pulled away from the embassy roof—that was the image many people had of the United States as a result of our failure to commit ourselves fully to that conflict.

The detente mentality was especially strong in American government during the 1971–79 period. It seemed to take over both parties. Every administration did its best to show the dictators of the USSR and China that we wanted to be friends. Both sides of the political aisle often appeared eager to cut military spending, give the communists fifty-year bank loans at low interest rates, and sign anything that could be called arms control. The simple fact of international life is that if people think they can take you, they will try.

During the Carter-Mondale administration we added another factor into our foreign relations: human rights.

I am still uncertain exactly what "human rights" refers to, but it came to play an almost paralyzing role in our relations with other nations throughout the world. In simple terms, a human-rights foreign policy means we only work with governments and let them be our friends if they do everything "right"—according to what we perceive as right.

Under this doctrine, it's sinful to work with a government that's not 100 percent pure. To further complicate things, the strongest and loudest proponents of human rights maintain a double standard about its application. Countries sympathetic to the United States are judged by a harsher rule than those countries hostile to capitalism and the American way of life.

We in Congress are repeatedly urged to end our support of governments fighting communist-supplied revolutionaries because of their human-rights violations. At the same time, however, we are told we must have a dialogue with the Kremlin and its puppets in Eastern Europe and Cuba; we are to expand trade and other relations so as to moderate their policies. The end result is that many nations who want to be our friends are driven toward the paws of the Soviet bear because we refuse to work with or even sell to them.

By my count, there have been at least six détentes between the United States and the Soviet Union. The result hasn't been a mellowing of Soviet expansionism, but more Soviet repression and imperialism. The tragedy of exported revolutions can be seen in Vietnam, Cambodia, Laos, Afghanistan, Angola, Mozambique, Ethiopia, South Yemen, and Nicaragua—to name only the most recent additions.

Despite all our efforts at expanded relations with the communists, where is freedom one bit better off today in Eastern Europe? Or in any Soviet puppet country? Does Poland have human rights? The tragic answer is that such a policy has only hurt our friends and helped our enemies, as the enslaved peoples of communist states tell us whenever they can.

By 1980, what America had achieved with pre emptive concessions and its human-rights policy was a world more dangerous and less free than it was twenty years ago. And the American people were tired of being humiliated. During the Carter-Mondale administration, our most noteworthy foreign-policy bright spot was the victory of the American hockey team over the Russians at the Lake Placid Olympics!

The election of Ronald Reagan represented a break with the policy of preemptive concessions and human rights at any price. Recognizing the importance of perception and images, the United States started to rebuild its military defenses. We raised the pay of America's servicemen and servicewomen, and moved toward a 600-ship navy to protect access to the sealanes of the world and vital mineral resources, which my colleague Henry Hyde discusses elsewhere in this book.

So don't let anyone tell you the Reagan policies haven't made a difference. During 1981–83 our real defense spending (meaning after inflation is taken into account) went up 39 percent. Of course we all hope our military power won't be needed, but as Winston Churchill once said, the best way to prevent war is to prepare for war. Being strong militarily costs money, but is there a more cost-effective way to spend money if the end result is to prevent war?

The test of leadership is results. *Since President Reagan has been in office, no country has gone communist.* In fact, in October 1983 we saw something we never saw before: a country under a communist dictatorship was brought back into the free world.

The rescue operation in Grenada, undertaken by the U.S. and six of its eastern Caribbean allies, was desperately needed. But you can bet it wouldn't have been tried under the Carter-Mondale administration.

Indeed, seven out of eight Democratic presidential candidates blasted President Reagan for his timely and courageous action—even *after* they could see how successful it had been. Their motto seems to be, "nothing fails like success."

These liberal candidates made light of the danger faced by 500 American medical students during the week before liberation. But it's better to be safe than sorry. There's a poster going around that asks, "What's the difference between a diplomat in Iran and a student in Grenada?" The answer is, "President Ronald Reagan."

The critics of the Grenada operation were amazed by the reaction of the American public. The people supported the president (by margins of two-to-one and higher) because for once *we had something to be proud of in international affairs.*

As a matter of fact, I recently was involved in discussions with some West German and British elected officials who told us privately that Grenada and the deployment of Pershing missiles in Western Europe were the greatest things America had done in a long while.

For Americans, Grenada brought us back some of our self-respect. Grenada also seved as a strong signal to

America's enemies that we will no longer allow our citizens to be threatened by communist elements; that the U.S. will keep peace and order in its own frontyard; and that Moscow and Havana will no longer subvert nations of this hemisphere without meeting strong resistance on our part.

But most important, Grenada confirmed a reality we must never forget: The advocates of communism *do not share our basic goals and values of peace, freedom and human dignity*—but they do understand the language of power.

If the United States takes a strong and vigilant stand for peace through strength, we'll avoid the tragedy of another major war and the potential loss of our independence. We'll have both peace *and* freedom.

If we fail in this, little else will really matter. All the debates that rage over how best to achieve a humane society and opportunity for all will be hollow and without purpose.

Yes, preparedness is expensive, terribly expensive. But is there a sensible and realistic alternative? We must pay the price of freedom! We owe ourselves and our children no less.

The Cliché

"Nuclear war is the biggest danger humanity faces, but all conservatives do is buy more weapons."

Conservatives worry too much about the Soviet Union's military spending. Hysterical talk about the Russians does more harm than good. It encourages us to spend more on defense than we can afford. The real danger is not being number two; it's that kind of thinking by us and the Soviets that could trigger nuclear war. Conservatives seem to be against arms control; they don't have any plan for pushing back the threat of nuclear holocaust. That makes them part of the problem rather than part of the solution.

10

Do Old Weapons Still Keep the Peace?

By Dan Crane, MC

I do solemnly swear that I will support and defend the Constitution of the United States against all enemies, foreign and domestic; that I will bear true faith and allegiance to the same; that I take this obligation freely, without any mental reservation or purpose of evasion; and that I will well and faithfully discharge the duties of the office on which I am about to enter. So help me God.

Federal Oath of Office

The first official act of every member of Congress is to pledge to "support and defend the Constitution" and to "bear true faith and allegiance" to it.

Among the primary responsibilities assigned to Congress by the Constitution (Article I, Section 8)—and thus a primary responsibility of each member of Congress—is to "provide for the common defense."

The instructions to Congress are clear. Members of Congress, in vowing to uphold the Constitution, are solemnly pledging to do all in their power to protect America.

Yet that defense has steadily eroded in recent years as Congress has turned its attention elsewhere. In fact, defense spending as a percentage of the federal budget was less under President Carter than at any time in the preceding forty years!

No responsible observer would make the claim that the U.S. still enjoys the military superiority we did as late as 1970. While this country has developed not a single major weapons system in many years, the Soviet Union has engaged in a crash military buildup unparalleled in history. In fact, during the decade 1974–83, Soviet military spending exceeded ours by approximately 40 percent. We will spend approximately 7.5 percent of our gross national product on the military by the end of the 1980s; the Soviets will spend 17 to 19 percent of theirs. (See figures 1 and 2.)

Those who insist the Soviets build weapons only because we do have no explanation for this massive arms program. But those who understand the nature of the Soviet empire need only let the facts speak.

You may be thinking, if we respond to the Soviet buildup by beefing up our own defenses, that will just increase the risk of war. That's a common assumption. Unfortunately,

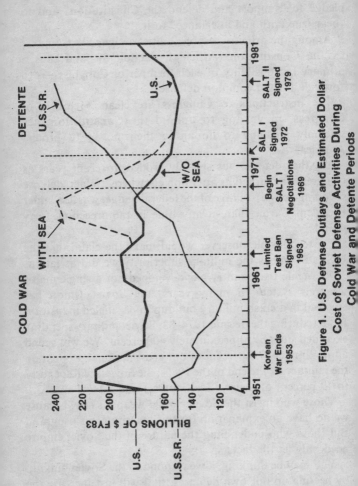

Figure 1. U.S. Defense Outlays and Estimated Dollar Cost of Soviet Defense Activities During Cold War and Detente Periods

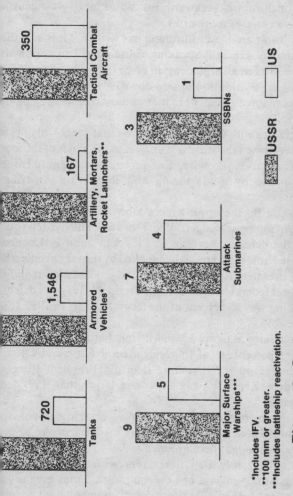

Figure 2. Comparison of Average Annual Soviet Production and FY 1985 U.S. Requests

*Includes IFV.
**100 mm or greater.
***Includes battleship reactivation.

USSR
US

Tanks 720

Armored Vehicles* 1,546

Artillery, Mortars, Rocket Launchers** 167

Tactical Combat Aircraft 350

Major Surface Warships*** 9 / 5

Attack Submarines 7 / 4

SSBNs 3 / 1

the conclusion is backward: instead of more arms causing war, war causes more arms.

As historian James Burnham has written, "It is said that armaments, generally speaking, cause wars. This notion, the logical crux of all arguments in favor of disarmament, turns the causal relationship upside-down. Actually, it is wars, or conflicts threatening war, that cause armaments, not the reverse."

Agreeing with George Washington that peace will only be achieved when the strongest army is in the hands of the most peaceful nation, President Reagan has taken steps to ensure that peace by modernizing and improving America's defenses.

Of course, the appeasement lobby howled at President Reagan's defense budget. What those folk failed to tell you is that the defense spending of President John F. Kennedy (whose name is reverentially invoked by the very people who vilify President Reagan's defense budget) was *almost half* of the total federal budget in 1962. President Reagan's defense spending was 26 percent of the federal budget in 1982. (See figure 3.)

By looking at figure 3, you will find that JFK spent a much greater percentage of the budget on defense and a lesser percentage on social welfare than did President Reagan. President Kennedy's tax cuts were larger than President Reagan's.

Many members of Congress, however, refuse to vote for the substantial sums required to modernize our armed forces. Although there are men today flying the very same planes their *fathers* flew, liberal representatives simply won't approve the purchase of new equipment. Some even argue that defense spending is the cause of our unbalanced budget.

Is it? Look at figure 4, which traces the federal budget debt from 1960 to 1982 and compares it with defense spending

88

Figure 8. Kennedy vs. Reagan Defense Spending

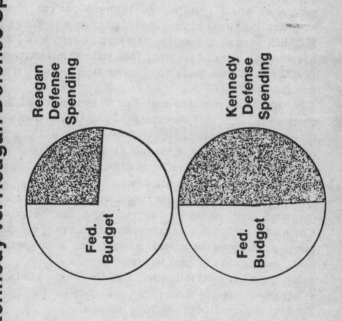

Reagan
Defense
Spending

Fed.
Budget

Kennedy
Defense
Spending

Fed.
Budget

You would think that if defense spending were responsible for budget deficits, then as defense spending fell, deficits would shrink. But the opposite is the case: as defense spending has been cut, total government debt has *risen*. That's because nondefense spending is responsible for our serious budget problems.

The real explosion in federal spending has been in social programs, which mushroomed from 25 percent of the budget in 1962 to 53 percent in 1982 (see figure 5). We spent $120 billion *more* on social welfare than on defense in 1982. Spending on just one program, food stamps, has increased 16,000 percent (no, that's not a misprint; it's a full sixteen thousand percent)!

None of this is meant to imply that we should give a blank check to the Pentagon, any more than we should eliminate those programs that help the truly needy. We in Congress have the responsibility to provide for the nation's defense, but we must exercise that responsibility with the utmost restraint. We must be "cheap hawks."

One reason I wanted to become a member of the investigations panel of the House Armed Service Committee was to prove that conservatives can apply their penny-pinching to the Pentagon too. I want to ensure that every single dollar is spent wisely.

If you are like most folk, you shared the country's outrage at reports of flagrant waste of tax dollars by the Pentagon. Some of the mind-boggling items included:

- $639 for a washer that should cost under $1
- $1,118 for a $1 plastic cap for a stool leg
- $109 for a 4-cent diode
- $54.75 for a gear and pinion that formerly cost $3.7

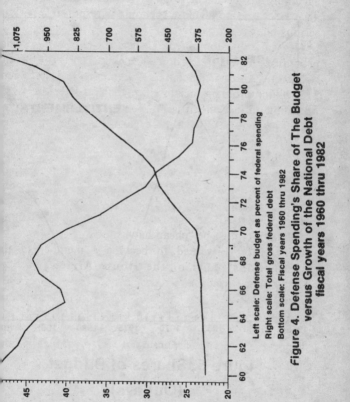

Left scale: Defense budget as percent of federal spending

Right scale: Total gross federal debt

Bottom scale: Fiscal years 1960 thru 1982

Figure 4. Defense Spending's Share of The Budget
versus Growth of the National Debt
fiscal years 1960 thru 1982

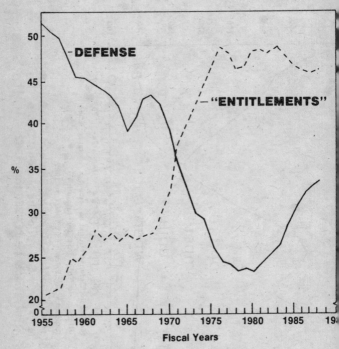

Figure 5. Shares of Budget
(Outlays)

92

Figure 6. Program to End Spare-Parts Price Abuse

1. Incentives for employees to find cost savings.
2. Stern disciplinary action against employees allowing abuses to continue.
3. Senior management to alert contractors to the seriousness of the problem and our strong resolve to control prices.
4. Services to make the competition advocate program work.
5. Services to refuse to pay unjustified price increases.
6. Services to seek refunds where overcharges have occurred.
7. Services to cease doing business with contractors refusing to meet our contracting standards.
8. Reforms in our basic contract procedures.
9. Additional audits and investigations.
10. Secretary's personal resolve to straighten up the spare-parts situation.

We must stop such unethical extravagance (see figure 6). Interestingly, it took a Republican administration to discover and publicize these abuses, some of which have been going on for decades.

Upon taking office, the Reagan administration discovered that our outdated defense procurement system failed to take advantage of competition and contained few incentives to cut costs or improve efficiency. A wide-ranging management reform program was started, including a thorough audit to identify waste and inefficiency, and a program to make the Defense Department follow sound business practices.

The department's work with the Justice Department in prosecuting those who defraud the government is paying off in recovering taxpayers' dollars (see figure 7). This enforcement program should also deter future fraud.

There is no inconsistency in advocating the strongest possible defense of our nation while clamping down hard on waste, fraud, and abuse. In fact, there is a special responsibility resting upon every individual advocating peace through strength. That duty is to ensure that the taxpayers' money and trust are wisely handled. After all, our goal is to defend the country, not offend the taxpayers.

As we move closer to the twenty-first century, we move nearer to making a dream the reality: the elimination of nuclear war. This is not at all as unrealistic as it may at first seem. The technology to bring it about exists right now.*

Suppose that instead of protecting our nation with nuclear missiles, we did it with a *non*nuclear shield? And further suppose that this nonnuclear defense could actually *prevent* a nuclear war from beginning?

This system would consist of a satellite network capable of

---

* Our nation owes a debt of gratitude to Lt. Gen. Daniel O. Graham (ret.) for his tireless efforts in behalf of the "high-frontier" concept.

Figure 7. Activities to Curb Waste, Fraud, and Abuse

Audits of Internal Management of Defense Operations and Programs

18,467 Reports

18,467 Reports

Potential Saving: $1.6 Billion

Potenial Saving: 1.6 Billion

Investigative Cases

16,357 Cases Closed

8,023 Cases Referred for Prosecution or Administrative Action

657 Convictions

Fines, Penalties, Restitutions, and Recoveries Collected for Referrals to:

Justice Department: $5.2 Million

Military Department: $9.6 Million

DCAA Audits

57,782 Reports

$28.6 Billion in Contract Costs Questioned $9.1 Billion Sustained intercepting and destroying incoming hostile missiles, and a backup network of small ground-based nonnuclear rockets.

Figures 8–10 show how the satellite defense would work.

If any incoming missiles managed to evade the satellites, the second layer of ground-based nonnuclear rockets would be activated, as shown in figures 11–13.

This alternative to the specter of a never-ending arms race deserves every American's careful consideration.

We face the most important decisions of our lives. As we work toward the establishment of permanent peace, we should remember that the man who said, "My first wish is to see this plague of mankind, war, banished from the earth," also advised us how to achieve this goal: "To be prepared for war is the most effectual means of preserving peace." The man was George Washington.

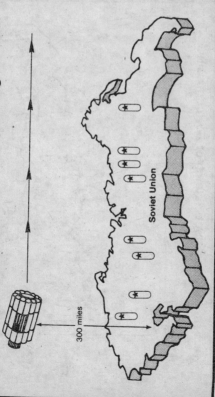

One of 432 armed satellites constantly circling the earth

300 miles

Soviet Union

FIG. 8. The illustration left portrays just one of 432 armed satellites in orbit to provide an active missile defense of the United States.

A web of 432 satellites would constantly circle the globe with some 100 of them in position over the Soviet Union at any given time at an altitude of three hundred miles and would provide a defensive blanket for America against all Soviet missile sites.

The armed satellites would provide America a new layer of defense by intercepting and destroying any offensive Soviet missile that has a trajectory into space, and do that over the Soviet Union.

The offensive Soviet missile would be spotted by infrared sensors while its exhaust still appears hot against the cold background of space.

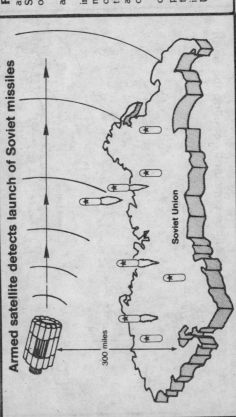

Armed satellite detects launch of Soviet missiles

300 miles

Soviet Union

FIG. 9. The illustration left shows an armed satellite positioned over the Soviet Union detecting the launch of an offensive Soviet missile.

Each armed satellite will carry fuel and be able to maneuver itself in space.

The armed satellite will be cylindrical in shape and house 40 to 45 self-propelled missiles attached to the satellite by a coupling mechanism designed to release the missiles into space so that they can also position themselves and then lock onto their targets.

Each satellite would have advanced computer systems, capable of independently commanding and controlling the launch of each of its 40 to 50 missiles in order to intercept an attack against the United States.

98

FIG. 10. The illustration left shows one armed satellite destroying several offensive Soviet missiles in the early part of their trajectory.

Each of the 40 to 45 missiles carried by each satellite would have two segments, one a booster, and the other a kill vehicle.

The kill vehicle would be propelled towards its target by the booster, and then released after the kill vehicles infrared guidance system has locked onto the Soviet missile.

The kill vehicle will be non-nuclear, and capable of obtaining a velocity of 3,000 to 6,000 feet per second.

The interceptors would impact the Soviet missiles at such incredible speed (almost 20,000 miles per hour) that even the impact of something as small as a nice cube could destroy the warhead of a ballistic missile.

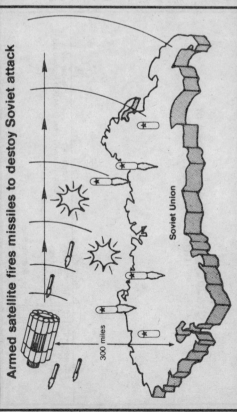

Armed satellite fires missiles to destoy Soviet attack

300 miles

Soviet Union

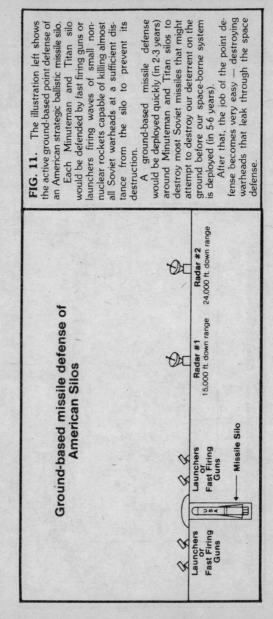

FIG. 11. The illustration left shows the active ground-based point defense of an American strategic ballistic missile silo.

Each Minuteman and Titan silo would be defended by fast firing guns or launchers firing waves of small non-nuclear rockets capable of killing almost all Soviet warheads at a sufficient distance from the silo to prevent its destruction.

A ground-based missile defense would be deployed quickly (in 2-3 years) around Minuteman and Titan silos to destroy most Soviet missiles that might attempt to destroy our deterrent on the ground before our space-borne system is deployed (in 5-6 years).

After that, the job of the point defense becomes very easy — destroying warheads that leak through the space defense.

Ground-based missile defense of American Silos

Launchers or Fast Firing Guns

Launchers or Fast Firing Guns

Missile Silo

Radar #1
15,000 ft. down range

Radar #2
24,000 ft. down range

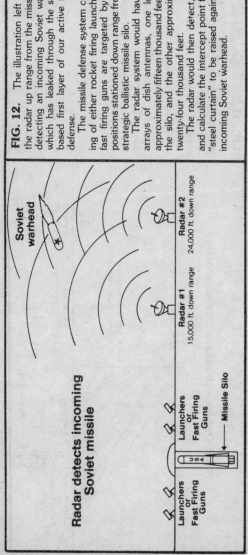

Radar detects incoming Soviet missile

Soviet warhead

Radar #1
15,000 ft. down range

Radar #2
24,000 ft. down range

Launchers
or
Fast Firing
Guns

Launchers
or
Fast Firing Guns

Missile Silo

U S A

FIG. 12. The illustration left shows the radar up range from the missile silo detecting an incoming Soviet warhead which has leaked through the satellite based first layer of our active missile defense.

The missile defense system consisting of either rocket firing launchers or fast firing guns are targeted by radar positions stationed down range from the strategic ballistic missile silo.

The radar system would have two arrays of dish antennas, one located approximately fifteen thousand feet from the silo, and the other approximately twenty-four thousand feet.

The radar would then detect, track and calculate the intercept point for the "steel curtain" to be raised against the incoming Soviet warhead.

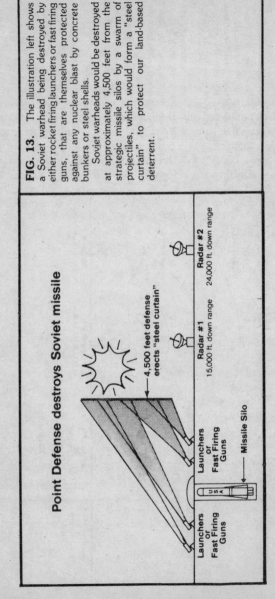

FIG. 13. The illustration left shows a Soviet warhead being destroyed by either rocket firing launchers or fast firing guns, that are themselves protected against any nuclear blast by concrete bunkers or steel shells.

Soviet warheads would be destroyed at approximately 4,500 feet from the strategic missile silos by a swarm of projectiles, which would form a "steel curtain" to protect our land-based deterrent.

Point Defense destroys Soviet missile

4,500 feet defense erects "steel curtain"

Launchers or Fast Firing Guns

Launchers or Fast Firing Guns

Missile Silo

Radar #1
15,000 ft. down range

Radar #2
24,000 ft. down range

The Cliché

*"America is a rich nation and should
spend more to help other countries."*

Conservatives are shortsighted on foreign aid. President
Carter doubled our foreign-aid spending, but President
Reagan's first three budgets cut it back by over 20 percent. If
conservatives support foreign aid at all, it's military or has
strings attached; they prefer military aid to the good-faith
economic-development grants that make nations prosperous
and more friendly to us. America owes the world more help
than conservatives are willing to give it, and we shouldn't play
politics or war games with that help.

11

What Kind of Foreign Aid Helps?

By Henry J. Hyde, MC

Americans, especially those west of the Boston–Washington corridor, are still largely isolationist and mistrust what
Jefferson called "foreign entanglements." Therefore, a sure
way to raise their blood pressure is to speak favorably about
foreign aid. Nevertheless, it is useful to analyze why some
hostility to this subject may be shortsighted, and to propose
some courses of action.

Because it is no longer possible to immunize our own
economy from the fiscal illnesses of other countries, we

ignore them at our peril. The rise of OPEC should have taught us that the oil prices less developed countries must pay will ultimately be reflected at the gas pump at our neighborhood service station.

We like to think that when America sneezes the rest of the world catches a cold, but the reverse is just as likely.

Moreover, while most of us weren't paying much attention, our economy became increasingly dependent on overseas markets. Today about 20 percent of U.S. industrial output is for export, and thus involves one of every six workers engaged in production. Farmers, perhaps more than any other single economic group, understand only too well that *two of every five acres produce for export*. About one-third of American corporate profits come from international activities.

Beyond the merely economic, there are strategic and geopolitical reasons for us to develop markets for our exports, and to ensure access to raw materials not available here.

Indeed, we are seriously mineral-dependent, and this has a direct relationship not only to the vigor of our industrial economy, but to national security as well. Table 1 illustrates this dependence, as well as underscores not only our need to have access to these vital raw materials (for economic as well as national security reasons), but also the companion need to have the sea lanes open to ensure access.

The inefficiencies of some U.S. foreign-aid programs, and the inability of foreign assistance to generate the support in Congress for regular authorizations and appropriations, give conservatives a chance to influence the direction of these programs.

As recently as summer 1983, conservatives on the Commission on Security and Economic Assistance

104

Carlucci commission) showed that there are alternatives to the "conventional wisdom" on foreign aid. I believe most conservatives will support foreign-assistance programs if they are in our national interest (as measured by agreed-upon foreign-policy goals) and if they offer citizens of other countries an opportunity to prosper in a climate of economic growth and free enterprise.

What's wrong with the conventional wisdom that has driven foreign aid for at least twenty years? It assumes that there is a finite amount of wealth in the world and that the West (or the Northern Hemisphere) has more than its fair share. The theory is that the wealthy countries acquired their wealth by exploiting the people and resources of poorer countries, and so we ought to feel guilty about our affluence. In other words, we owe them.

The less developed countries demand the transfer of resources from the wealthy northern to the impoverished southern countries to build a "fairer" economic world order. The consequence is that taxpayers in successful countries have to bleed for the "crime" of success.

If there is a dominant theme in the United Nations, it is that third-world poverty exists because of European colonialism, and is perpetuated by the greed of the industrialized nations. The nastiest enemy is capitalism.

Much Latin American animosity toward the United States can be assigned to scapegoating—blaming someone else for one's domestic difficulties. Despite the Good Neighbor Policy of Roosevelt, and Kennedy's Alliance for Progress, poverty is still the reality for too many Latin Americans.

But American taxpayers question whether the U.S. can endlessly respond to this when our resources are finite and evidence shows that our interventions don't often work.

Table 1
U.S. Net Import Reliance for Strategic and Critical Nonfuel Minerals—1982 (in percentages)
For Those 26 Materials with Net Import Reliance over 50%

Mineral	Major Foreign Source	% of Net Imports	Total Net Imports	Major Usage
Asbestos	Canada	97%	74%	Friction products.
	South Africa	3		
Barite	China	24	52	Over 90 percent used as a weighting agent in oil- and gas-well drilling fluids.
	Peru	21		
	Chile	13		
Bauxite	Jamaica	40	97	Bauxite and alumina are ores used primarily to produce aluminum.
	Guinea	28		
	Australia	76		
Alumina	Jamaica	15		
Cadmium	Canada	27	69	Coating and plating
	Australia	18		
	Mexico	11		

Chromite	South Africa	44	
	USSR	18	
	Philippines	12	
Ferrochromium	South Africa	71	Chromite and ferrochromium used to harden
	Yugoslavia	11	88	steel alloys and produce stainless-steel products.
Cobalt	Zaire	38	
	Zambia	13	91	Mainly for construction of industrial and aircraft gas turbine engines.
Columbium	Brazil	73	
	Canada	6	100	End uses as metal and alloys in fabricated form.
Corundum	South Africa	100	100	With optical components.
Diamond*	Ireland	57	
	South Africa	15	100	Primarily, drilling industry.
Fluorspar	Mexico	60	
	South Africa	30	87	Aluminum, fluorchemical, and uranium industries.
Gallium	Switzerland	65	
	Canada	12	
	West Germany	10	61	Over 90 percent of gallium consumed was for electronic applications.

Gem stones**	South Africa	29	
	Belgium–Luxembourg	23	
	Israel	21	100	Jewelry and industrial.
Graphite (natural)	Mexico	60	
	South Korea	12	100	Refractories, steel production, foundry operations.
Ilmenite	Australia	59	
	Canada	34	
	South Africa	6	72	Pigment products, welding coatings, metal, alloys.
Manganese ore	Gabon	32	
	South Africa	24	
	Australia	18	99	Steel production, pig iron, dry-cell batteries, and various chemical uses.
Mica sheet (natural)	India	83	
	Brazil	11	100	Primarily in manufacture of electrical and electronic equipment.
Nickel	Canada	44	
	Norway	11	75	In production of stainless and alloy steel, nonferrous alloys, and electroplating.

Mineral	Country	%		Major uses
Platinum-group metals	South Africa USSR United Kingdom	56 16 11	85	Mainly as a catalyst by automotive, chemical, and petroleum refining industries.
Potash	Canada Israel	94 3	71	Primarily as fertilizer agent.
Selenium	Canada Japan	44 17	50	With electronic and photocopier components.
Silver	Canada Mexico	37 24	59	Photography, electrical, and electronic products.
Strontium	Mexico	99	100	Pyrotechnics and signals, ferrite ceramic permanent magnets, purifying electrolytic zinc.
Tantalum	Thailand Canada	38 11	90	In production of metal, powders, ingots, fabricated forms, and compounds with following end uses: electronic components, machinery, and transportation industry.
Tin	Malaysia Thiailand Bolivia	39 21 17		

Commodity	Country			Major uses
	Indonesia	13	72	Major use in electrical, construction, transportation, and containers.
Zinc (metal)	Canada	51	53	Galvanizing, zinc-base alloy, brass, and bronze. Coproducts of zinc are lead, cadmium, silver, and copper.
	Spain	8		
Zinc (ore and concentrates)	Canada	59		
	Peru	17		

SOURCE: 1983 Mineral Commodity Summaries, Department of the Interior, Bureau of Mines. Resource information by Geological Survey.

* Industrial stone.
** Diamond imports were about 84 percent of total.

110

Those of us who support foreign aid have a rough time making the case for aid programs with so little to show for them.

What's worse, the economic failures we are called to address often result from the socialist economies of the third-world nations themselves. Africa, as a continent, until recently produced enough food to feed its people and even provide surpluses. Independence for many African states, however, brought to power socialist revolutionaries who hate free enterprise.

The result has been wholesale starvation, which often provides the revolutionary leaders with a license to steal, since more and more state-run operations depend on price controls and subsidies to keep the poor quiet. Many Americans see foreign-aid programs as simply bailing out socialist failures abroad and thus perpetuating them.

The January 16, 1984, issue of *Time* magazine discusses the history of Africa's human-rights abuses and misgovernment. In rural Senegal a $250,000 U.S.-made solar-powered irrigation system is idle because of no maintenance. In Zambia hundreds of government vehicles sit in a parking lot, lacking a spare part or two. *Time* says the government of President Kaunda prefers importing new vehicles through aid programs to purchasing spare parts to fix the old ones.

These are but two examples of indefensible waste in so many of our foreign-aid programs in the underdeveloped world. The need is certainly there; the programs are there; but the results too often are waste and more waste.

Grenada is another good example. Not only did its former leader Maurice Bishop cozy up to Fidel Castro, but he instituted strict, centralized controls over the economy. After Bishop's murder by an even more radical clique, the United States joined other Caribbean states to boot out the Cuban, North Korean, and East European communist gangsters who thought they had found another beachhead in our backyard.

Recently, officials of the U.S. Agency for International Development (AID), our main economic assistance agency, have been debating whether to build free-market institutions in Grenada. A number of bureaucrats are arguing against any tinkering with socialistic institutions already established by Bishop and his now exterminated Marxist-Leninist clique.

My point here is simple: *conservatives can probably support foreign economic assistance if it is conditional.* In Grenada and elsewhere, U.S. foreign aid should establish private, for-profit institutions that will flourish after we end our assistance. It must not be seem to be endless.

What does it take to develop conservative support for foreign economic assistance? Except for things like famines or earthquakes, assistance ought to advance U.S. foreign-policy goals in a country; virtually every dollar spent on foreign aid ought to be conditioned on policy reforms that hold out a real hope for ultimate prosperity.

I happen to be an optimist. Prosperity is attainable in most countries of the world; and the United States, through foreign economic assistance, ought to help *generate* wealth rather than merely transfer it.

Recently, the new members of the Board of Directors of the Inter-American Foundation named a new president. The IAF is an autonomous public corporation established by Congress in 1969 to carry out new assistance programs aimed at large groups of disadvantaged people in Latin America and the Caribbean region, groups overlooked by conventional foreign aid. Great leeway was granted the foundation; its funding was provided by congressional appropriations and from funds supplied by a U.S. trust administered by the Inter-American Development Bank.

112

The foundation has acted quickly and at times effectively, but also without appropriate oversight.

In hearings this year by two subcommittees of the House Foreign Affairs Committee, the proudest boast of the foundation's backers was that its programs were not tied to the foreign policy of the United States. This arrangement may satisfy the liberal think-tanks in Washington, but it cannot satisfy the American taxpayer paying for the programs. And since United States tax dollars are supporting these programs, the latter should not go against U.S. foreign policy.

Perhaps it is too idealistic to expect gratitude, but recipients of U.S. generosity ought to be friendly to the United States. Recent news stories tell of a $40 million foreign-aid proposal for Robert Mugabe's Zimbabwe, down from the proposed $75 million. What triggered this change of policy was the Zimbabwean regime's sponsorship of a U.N. resolution that condemned the Caribbean–U.S. rescue mission in Grenada. Prime Minister Mugabe had the *chutzpah* to complain about the aid cut a few days after joining his socialist third-world compatriots in that vote. This, mind you, is the country that could not bring itself to vote for a U.S. resolution in the United Nations deploring the Soviets' shooting down of South Korean airliner KAL 007 last year.

Let's redefine what we mean in the Foreign Assistance Act by "allies" worthy of U.S. assistance. Most conservatives deem redefinition as a *minimum* step. We must not continue to assist so-called nonaligned states that live in holy terror of siding with the United States. Maybe we can't alter the attitudes or behavior of other countries, but we can stop subsidizing them.

An extension of this argument would be to deny assistance to any regime using foreign troops to keep itself in power.

113

We certainly should shut off the flow of aid dollars to those countries where the Soviets, Cubans, and Libyans substitute force for elections and prop up tottering regimes.

Some will say that this is too sweeping. They tell us that harsh measures only "drive them more deeply into the Soviets' arms." This argument didn't hold water in Sandinista-dominated Nicaragua, or earlier in Cuba, and it doesn't make sense today.

Many difficulties in foreign aid come from the "bureaucratic reward system." Bureaucrats are often evaluated by their ability to "push the product." This is true in the field and in Washington. The push to create projects to provide gold stars for career bureaucrats should be halted.

A basic reform would return much more project control to Washington, D.C., or, alternatively, provide more oversight from Washington. Congress, which loves to create agencies and pass appropriations to solve problems, ought occasionally to scrutinize an agency's work.

Those of us on the Carlucci commission were reminded that much of the money spent on foreign aid is, in fact, spent in this country. Further, we were urged to remember that the U.S. is really ungenerous, given world need, and that our aid program is small compared with what Americans spend on entertainment or cosmetics.

But people buy these products as free consumers. Foreign assistance, however, is funded either by your tax dollars or by borrowing.

Clearly, most programs ought to be *bilateral.* Between a recipient country and the United States, decisions can be made that will benefit those receiving the assistance as well as U.S. taxpayers. (There is a role for international lending agencies, but given scarce economic resources, let's invest primarily in bilateral and multilateral programs that we and the beneficiary can keep tabs on.)

114

One recommendation of the Carlucci commission is useful to conservatives. Since at least the mid-1970s, aid-dispensing agencies have broken up the world into sectors, such as housing, education, population, or health. This has been done with little regard to the total requirements of a recipient country.

We must halt funding programs that ignore the overall needs of a country. We ought to encourage growth and prosperity. To go on endlessly funding the failed socialism of so many third-world countries doesn't make sense.

The Carlucci commission proposed a "country approach" to foreign economic and military assistance. A country is much more than the sum of its sectors. By advocating land reform, we may be discouraging the production of more food. The culture and traditions of a country must be included in our calculations, because if we are too aggressive in seeking to impose our values, such as imposing a new role for women, we may cause social strife. By seeing only hungry mouths while ignoring the availability of willing hands, we perpetuate dependence.

Economic assistance ought not to go primarily to governments. Too often, field employees have pet ministries (relating to sectors) that they want to enhance. We need to have private, market-oriented expertise available to overseas businesses in exactly the way state universities are used to supply direct technical assistance to farmers.

How much better it would be to have American businesses of all sizes providing direct technical assistance in building free-enterprise counterparts, instead of sending American sociologists, anthropologists, economists, and "planners" to help governments be more pervasive and stifle growth and development.

The glue of international prosperity is trade. Our foreign economic programs should stress trade promotion. By encouraging free-trade zones, investment of foreign capital, low taxes, and nonprotectionism, and by providing investors with guarantees against expropriation, developing countries can grow the way Singapore, South Korea, and Taiwan have done.

Unfortunately, foreign-aid bureaucrats are often hostile to international development through trade. The Overseas Private Investment Corporation and others can do only so much. We must do better.

In this chapter I have discussed nine points that should bring greater conservative support for foreign-assistance programs:

1. Tying foreign aid to long- and short-term U.S. foreign-policy goals
2. Emphasizing free-enterprise institutional development and economic growth
3. Linking assistance to international behavior and making all aid conditional
4. Centralizing management and planning of aid programs in Washington
5. Emphasizing bilateral, rather than multilateral, assistance
6. Conducting fairer, less biased assessments of aid effectiveness
7. Adopting a "country" approach to aid requirements instead of "sectoral" one
8. Phasing out foreign governments as recipients, and emphasizing private-sector implementation within a country
9. Emphasizing development of free trade and international commerce

The Reagan administration has brought a new realism to foreign aid, and Americans ought not to shy from a much bolder application of these reforms.

For the most part I have stressed economic support, but often military support is essential to protect the economic development within a country.

In El Salvador we have given three dollars in economic assistance for every dollar of military assistance, but the latter is needed to protect the former—the Marxist guerrillas practice hit-and-run tactics to bomb bridges, power plants, and other infrastructures. These must be militarily protected so the economic aid is not wasted.

Let's start using American money to bring about positive, long-lasting change in the world. We can achieve this by going beyond the old-fashioned debate of foreign aid based on liberal precepts versus no foreign aid at all.

The modern conservative approach to foreign aid means we demand *results* while we promote *freedom*. If we do things right, America will have more friends throughout the world, and our nation will be more secure.

When it comes to a smart approach to foreign aid, we owe it not nearly so much to the world as to the people who are paying the bills—the American taxpayers.

The Cliché

"Republicans talk about housing reform, but their reforms throw the needy out into the street."

Republicans want to take their budget meat ax to the housing programs of the federal government. They resent the liberal efforts of the last several decades, which have been a huge success in housing the poor and the lower middle class. They talk about helping more people with fewer tax dollars by using individual initiative and the free market, but there's no evidence this will work. Don't take Republicans seriously when they talk about reforming housing programs.

12

Can Housing the Poor Be Done Better?

By John Hiler, MC

To be a Republican in a Democratic Congress and to propose a better way of providing housing assistance is like walking around an archery contest with an apple on your head. All the archers know the point of the match is to shoot at the target with the big painted rings. Yet for some reason, the romantic allure of the apple is just too much. Lose though they may, some would rather go for the apple.

In 1972 the Department of Housing and Urban Development began an experiment to see if its housing programs could be replaced by a housing "voucher system." The Experimental Housing Allowance Program conducted tests in twelve cities with 30,000 households across the nation. Over 300 technical reports—enough to build a house—analyzed the program into oblivion.

The conclusion was clear: By giving housing assistance payments to participants and letting them select their own housing, the government could *help house almost twice as many people.* Based on the success of the program, HUD and the president's Commission on Housing said the government should use a voucher system in the place of existing assistance programs.

The response from the Democratic Congress befuddled the mind. Liberals said the administration and its supporters in Congress were really trying to wreck programs designed to provide decent housing for the poor. To prevent that from happening, Congress authorized *more* money for *more* "development" programs and again committed tax dollars to twenty-year contracts for the more expensive Section 8 Existing Housing program.

Despite the data from the housing voucher experiment and ignoring the success of the program, Congress authorized *yet another* allowance "demonstration" project—*to the tune of $242,115,000.*

This strange compulsion to shoot at apples is curious but not uncommon with the other party. If a Republican proposes a new and better social program, Democrats shift their sights away from the real targets, bellowing all the while about fairness and protecting the poor from the ravages of change.

Just as certain is their unshakable defense of the liberal

welfare state, a structure put up oh, so many years ago when conditions were oh, so very different.

The truth is that a housing voucher system *can help more people* (isn't that the point?) more efficiently, and still offer freedom of choice. Yet judging by the odd reaction from the liberal camp, one would think housing vouchers could serve only to shove the poor out into the cold of night. Nonsense. It's just that many liberals still dearly believe that only *they* can help the poor. Well, the housing voucher program proves them wrong. Simply put, the Republicans' proposal is right on target.

Sally Jackson* once lived in subsidized housing—"the projects," she called them—for five years. Sally was divorced, jobless, and raising two young children; her entire income was $238 per month from Aid to Families with Dependent Children (AFDC), one of the government's main "income-security" programs. Each month Sally paid $50 as her part of the rent for her government-owned and government-built apartment. The rest of the rent was paid with tax dollars.

The projects Sally describes were not slums. Murderers, thieves, and cockroaches did not terrorize the halls and streets. The apartments had just been built, and Sally liked them all right.

But Sally also says that living in subsidized housing "tends to breed an uncertainty. There is no help-your-neighbor attitude. There is constant anxiety." She uses the image of falling down, and how people around you in the projects just don't help you up. You just lie there.

* Not her real name, by her request. "Sally" did agree to respond to questions about statements made for this chapter. Dorothea T. Miller, whose story is told later, also exists, and that *is* her real name.

120

"Have you ever been to a project?" Sally asks. "You're constantly looking over your shoulder."

Sally says it's hard to get ahead when you live in the projects because "people assume that when you live in a project, it's negative." If you want a job, if you want a loan to help you get ahead, you have to show some stability, Mrs. Jackson says. As long as you live in subsidized housing, as long as your income comes from the government, you don't have that. More important to Sally, though, is the fact that "kids need stability."

Sally washed the walls of her government-owned apartment when she left the projects to join the housing-allowance program.

South Bend, Indiana, one of the cities I represent in the Third District, was part of the housing-allowance experiment. The experiment lasted ten years, but a five-year extension was granted to phase out the program more gracefully. About 26,000 people were helped during the ten-year period.

As tested in South Bend, a housing allowance gave qualified families direct cash payments to help with their rent, mortgage payments, or repair and upkeep costs. The apartment or home had to meet, or be repaired to meet, strict minimum standards of safety and livability. Other than that, people could choose *any existing apartment or home* in any location they preferred. If the unit cost more than the allowance, they made up the difference from their own income. If the apartment or house cost less, they could use the money for repairs or cosmetic changes.

The logic of the program is strong. Our nation experienced, from 1947 to 1974, an extremely high level of housing construction and an almost constant demand for new and better housing. The stock of existing housing, *good housing*, mushroomed. In the 1970s, inflation drove up new-home prices by some 147 percent.

Because of these new factors, the problem with housing low-income Americans was no longer the lack of units, as it had been during the depression and right after. The problem was affordability.

The best way to help provide adequate shelter for the poor, then, is not to build more units, as liberals often want to do, but to give cash help to lower-income families so they can afford the rents and mortgages of existing housing.

There are two reasonable ways of doing this. The first is the approach used in the Section 8 program so popular with Democrats. Here's how it works.

The government wants to help John Doe in Mainville, Illinois, rent an apartment. It must first find out how much apartments rent for there, so it conducts a survey of prices. From the study the government learns that a safe, decent apartment can be found for $200–$400.

Now, to make sure John does not spend too much of the government's money, a rent limit is set. John must find an apartment that costs *no more than* the limit.

The government also wants to make sure, however, that the rent limit is not too restrictive. If the limit is too low, John may not be able to find an apartment that suits his needs. Units for $200–$300 may be available, but they may be located a bit out of the way. Or perhaps at times only a few units in that price range are available; so, if John goes to rent one at the wrong time, none will be available. To make sure John can find an apartment, the government plays it safe by setting the maximum price John can spend at $350. In truth the government has been forced to create a buffer.

The cushion is all well and good—we want John to have a place to live—but by setting a limit and making the buffer necessary, it costs taxpayers more. Here's why.

First, the government is not going to pay the entire rent. Instead, John must contribute a certain percentage of his income—30 percent, by law—toward the cost of renting. If John makes $400 per month, then he must pay $120 out of his own pocket. The government's part, known as a subsidy, is the difference between John's contribution and the monthly rent. If the apartment costs $250, then the government pays $130. If the price is $350, then taxpayers subsidize John's rent by shelling out $100 more.

Because John spends the same amount of his own money whether the unit costs more or less, John *has no incentive to make an effort to find a less expensive apartment.* In fact, the opposite is true: he is inclined to lease a more expensive unit at more cost to the government. The only way to change this inclination is to lower the price limit. Yet this means the government must cut the buffer, and it is not inclined to do this.

Second, the government is not going to send the subsidy money to John. The money goes to the *landlord.* The landlord knows that the cost to John stays the same; so if he raises the price, all that happens is that he gets more money from the government.

Because the landlord is in business to rent apartments and make money and because John has no particular incentive to shop around and find a less costly unit, chances are good that the cost will be more, not less. The rule holds true: anytime you set a maximum allowable price, prices tend to rise to that level. The result? *More cost to the government and more cost to the taxpayer.*

What we need, then, is a system that ends the need for a cushion, provides John with an incentive to shop around, and takes away the landlord's inclination to charge a higher price. The method used in the voucher program does all this.

Let's go back to Mainville, where a good apartment can be

found for $200–$400. The government is still going to help John rent one, and the government is still going to determine how much it pays by subtracting John's contribution from the price of a good, decent unit.

This time, however, a maximum price is *not* set, and the subsidy payment is sent *directly to Mr. Doe,* not to the landlord. Watch what happens.

Because there is no maximum price, the government can shave off a good portion of the buffer. It knows that a less expensive unit can be found if John shops around. The government also knows that if the number of units in the price range drops, John can still rent: there is no price ceiling to keep him from spending a bit more of his own money for a while if he has to. So, the government can be more precise in deciding what a fair rent is in Mainville.

Let's say it decides on $250, and it sends a check directly to John for $130. Now John has all of the cash in his pocket, so if he pays $200 for an apartment, he is $50 ahead. If he wants a better unit, or if he doesn't want to bother with too much shopping, he can chip in a few more dollars of his own. That's his choice.

Yet the inclination, in this case, is to *shop more and spend less.* John's contribution is not going to stay the same, and the extra money comes out of his pocket. If an apartment house has good, inexpensive units but is a bit out of the way and a closer building rents units for more, John has an incentive to put the effort into going where they rent for less.

As far as the landlord is concerned, he knows John is probably looking for a good buy. If he prices apartments too high, Washington isn't going to cough up more money. John is—and he's not inclined to spend it. The incentive for landlords to bump up prices is gone.

The downward pressure on prices even works its way back

124

to justify lowering the buffer. Instead of having to add in a cushion because John and the landlord are inclined to go for higher prices, the government can now count on a *shopping factor* to help keep rent costs down.

In short, *John Doe has a perfectly good safe place to live and it has cost taxpayers less money.*

Sally Jackson, after washing her walls and leaving the projects, joined South Bend's Experimental Housing Allowance Program. Because "kids need stability, especially from a single-parent home," and because she wanted to get ahead, she used her money from AFDC and the $186 per month from the housing-allowance program to qualify for a mortgage.

She bought a modest home in a neighborhood where "the houses look the same as they did twenty years ago," and used an advance from the program to pay her utility deposit, paint the house, fix up the yard, and take care of a plumbing problem. The three-bedroom house is close to a busline, grocery stores, parks, and an elementary school.

Mrs. Jackson credits the program and the house it helped her buy with giving her a fair chance in life. She says that the "community looks at you differently—you're stable. It treats you like people." Had she stayed in the projects, she "wouldn't have had a chance." The housing-allowance program and her home "make it unlimited; the other's [government housing] limited."

When asked about the program ending in five years, Sally shows no fear: "In five years' time, why I could do *anything*. I will have a good job then; that will supplement for housing allowance."

Says Sally, "If you strip a person of dignity, you'd have a social revolution. It would be worse than a depression."

The housing-allowance program gave Mrs. Jackson and her children a real home, a chance to improve their lives—and dignity.

The South Bend results show how the housing-allowance program can help more people. In South Bend, the typical subsidy under Section 8 is currently $346 per month, or $4,152 per year. The administrative cost is $190 per recipient per year, for a total cost of $4,342. For the Experimental Housing Allowance Program, the cost is $240 per month, or $2,880 per year. Adding in the administrative cost of $163 per recipient per year, the total is $3,043, or $1,299 less per year. As a result, *one-third more people* can be helped by using the housing-allowance program.

The fact that both renters *and* homeowners were in the Experimental Housing Allowance Program adds even greater appeal. The old housing program was, and is, limited to renters. Allowing home*ownership,* however, increased freedom of choice, worked to restore homes and neighborhoods, offered families more mobility, allowed Sally Jackson to get ahead, and gave many participants, especially the elderly, the chance to get needed assistance without having to move—all at less expense than the Section 8 program.

Dorothea T. Miller has lived in her two-bedroom bungalow for thirty-five years. She is seventy-three years old. Her husband spent his life working for the YMCA, and when he died in 1975, all he left was the house and a small social-security stipend. It is Mrs. Miller's only income. The house sits in a comfortable, established neighborhood. "Nothing fancy," Mrs. Miller says.

Because Mr. Miller worked for the YMCA, a charitable organization, there was never very much money. They had to live on what little they had. But whatever the circumstances, her husband "had a great deal of pride in keeping the house up." After he died, the home began to look a bit run down.

Mrs. Miller gets $144 per month from the experimental housing program. With it, she put a new roof on the house, fixed her water heater, added storm doors to cut utility costs, and took care of other minor repairs.

"My friends tell me how much improved, how great it looks," she reports. "It helps to keep the neighborhood up to snuff."

The modest amount means she can stay in her home. Dorothea doubts she could afford an apartment by selling her home and investing the money. She is fairly certain she'd still need assistance of some kind.

Being alone and reaching the age when she has to think about getting from place to place, she also wonders about moving where the services she needs are "handy." Her house is "close to transportation, close to a place to shop, and close to a bank," making Dorothea's life much more comfortable and much more secure.

In passing the 1984 housing bill, Congress authorized $9.2 billion over the next twenty years for housing assistance to lower-income families, for modernizing government-built complexes, for "development" projects, and for moderate rehabilitation of existing units. This works out to be roughly $460 million per year, and Congress figures the amount will help house 85,000 people, apart from the voucher demonstration program.

However, by looking at those figures from the perspective of South Bend's experimental voucher program—the one that helped house people by providing an average annual assistance of $2,880—you find that the same $460 million could help 160,000 people, *almost twice as many*. From the other angle, Congress could help the same number of people (85,000) and cut the deficit by some $4.1 billion over the next twenty years.

For Sally Jackson, however, the housing-allowance program means more than budget numbers. Sally counts the $186 she receives each month only as an opportunity for her and her children. It means a chance to get off welfare and live in the kind of home children need if they are to do well in school and succeed. The assistance helped her buy a house, but it has also given her family something much more precious—dignity.

Dorothea T. Miller doesn't talk about the housing-allowance program in numbers either. She chats warmly about her thirty-five-year-old house, the home her children grew up in and the home her husband cared so much about. Living in that house means a more comfortable life for Mrs. Miller, and a program that can help a woman enjoy her golden years has a lot going for it.

The housing voucher program means adequate housing for Americans who can't afford it on their own, and it does this more efficiently than current housing programs. But as Sally and Dorothea know, the program also promises the opportunity to make their own choices, the chance to get ahead, and the means to improve the quality of life—less tangible, but more valuable, benefits.

Republicans continue to find and use commonsense approaches to helping fellow citizens who need it. The housing voucher program is but one example of that. Yet, so long as Democrats insist on turning away from the real target—helping people economically—and hurl arrows at Republicans, we will lose new and better programs to help the poor

It is vital that the Democrats focus less on Republicans. Arrows shot without a proper, painted target are dangerous things. Unaimed, they tend merely to sail on and on, unstopped, and uncaring of where they land. But land they do, and how tragic it is that the wounded may be the Sally Jacksons and Mrs. Millers of the world.

The Cliché

> *"America needs an industrial policy to preserve jobs, cut red tape, and raise competitiveness."*

Competition and individual enterprise served America well in the past, but what we need in the 1980s are cooperation and centralized leadership. A planning board, led by the best minds in government, business, and labor, can give the U.S. the industrial policy it needs. Federal loans and credits would go to the auto and steel industries, to keep them alive. The board would pick the winning technologies and products of tomorrow and get them started earlier. This will offset the waste and misdirection of the free-market system, and help us do better in world trade.

13

Should Bureaucrats Run Businesses?

By Dan Lungren, MC

Do you want your job security and prosperity set by a bureaucratic board in Washington?

Do you want the economic future of your children decided by a select panel in the nation's capital or should they be free to determine their jobs in the open marketplace?

If some in Congress have their way, most of our economic decisions will be made by a select sixteen-member panel.

After chairing a number of hearings for the Joint Economic Committee with witnesses ranging across the political spectrum, I have come to the conclusion that industrial policy would be one of the worst steps we could take.

Industrial-policy proponents think a council with sixteen board members from government, business, labor, and academia could do a better job of coordinating government policy to improve America's competitiveness.

Additionally, some in Congress hope to back up the council with a national bank. The bank would actually be a "government corporation," according to the statute language, able to make special loans, issue loan guarantees, or buy capital stock of selected industries.

Make no mistake: industrial policy as seen by its advocates is far different from present economic policy. It would be a radical departure from our present course, so severe that I believe it would mean a basic change in the political and economic structures of America.

The real irony is that, if enacted in this year of George Orwell's big brother, industrial policy would lead to big-brother central planning and intrusion into our lives.

The industrial-policy concept is based on several wrong notions. The first is that "the best and the brightest" are in Washington and that they can do a better job of making the economic decisions affecting our lives.

But countless examples show that government should stay out of planning when the marketplace does a better job. A few years ago we had petroleum price controls. People figured during a crisis government could allocate the petroleum we had in this country better than the marketplace.

I recall coming back to Washington after I'd been in my home district in Southern California, where we had long lines of people waiting to get gas. I talked with a congressman from Michigan on the floor of the House of Representatives. He told me that they were selling gas around the clock in Michigan; they had *plenty* of gas.

A member from Tennessee told me that they were having price wars in his state.

Why was it easier to get gas in some states and more difficult in others? Primarily because the government based allocation on the historical record. I have little doubt that the bureaucrats who set the petroleum allocation wanted to be fair. The problem with the historical record is that the marketplace changes *daily;* using historical data months and years old, the government was messing everything up with supplies not following contemporary demand.

Was this a result of a deliberate attempt to be unfair? No. Government wanted to be fair, but it simply can't do the job as well as the marketplace does.

The industrial policy some members of Congress are advocating would affect much more than gasoline. The main bill in the House of Representatives to create an industrial policy would "identify national economic problems [and] develop recommendations to address those problems." That is a very broad agenda.

For me to decide between adopting industrial policy and trying to improve the current marketplace is to choose between economic and individual freedom on the one hand and economic autocracy and Washington elitism on the other.

Donald T. Regan, secretary of the treasury, accurately stated, "The marketplace is...the dynamic interaction of millions of traders, customers, investors, business people. And it is...the most knowledgeable judge of economic winners and losers known to man." Admittedly, the marketplace has its imperfections and is not, nor should it

132

be, totally free from governmental influence. Nevertheless, the question of embarking upon a new industrial policy represents, said the treasury secretary, a choice "between having economic allocation decisions made by 230 million Americans acting in the free marketplace, and 20 to 30 government planners acting collectively in a political arena."

The truly frightening concern I have about industrial policy is that it presumes the government can do what few well-informed and successful entrepreneurs think *they* are capable of doing.

Robert Noyce, a coinventor of the integrated circuit and now vice chairman of Intel Corporation, told the Joint Economic Committee of the Congress not long ago: "I have great concern about [the government's] ability to pick winners and losers."

Noyce, elected to both the National Academy of Engineering and the National Academy of Science and awarded the National Medal of Science, told committee members a personal story.

"Since I have spent most of my life in the entrepreneurial high technology business, I should be better than most in picking winners and losers.

"Yet I advised my wife a few years ago not to invest in the local startup which has turned out to be the most successful in American industrial history to date—Apple Computer.

"It is precisely because those of us who should have known better but didn't see that opportunity, including, if I may say so, the big established computer companies that gave Apple such a big opportunity...[that] I'm afraid that kind of performance would be replicated in any committee decision on what we should invest in."

He added, "I'm fortunate that my wife, like most, did not take my advice."

Another failing of industrial policy is that it concentrates on reallocating *existing* resources to favored parts of the economy instead of focusing on progrowth policies where everyone can come out ahead. Industrial-policy advocates would have us fight over a limited economic pie, rather than bake a bigger pie.

Because of this fact, the unavoidable result of the industrial policy would be picking winners and losers. Industrial policy is designed to operate with stagnant resources; one enterprise would therefore inevitably be favored over another. *One entity would necessarily benefit at the expense of others.*

With experience serving as a guide, the council's help is likely to go to those firms with more political clout. Decisions that should be based on economics would instead be based on politics.

Senator William Proxmire (D-Wis.), writing on industrial policy, noted, "Money will go where the political power is. . . . It will go where union power is mobilized. It will go where the campaign contributors want it to go. It will go where the mayors and governors as well as congressmen and senators have the power to push it. Anyone who thinks government funds will be allocated to firms according to merit has not lived or served in Washington very long."

By virtue of its makeup, the proposed industrial-policy council would favor those groups serving on it—big business, big government, big labor, big academia. Adding it all up, bigness would be favored over small business and the individual. One has to wonder why it is that under the industrial-policy plan many of the most important elements of our economy would be left out of the picture.

Of course, if you have a lot of political clout, you may not have much to worry about under this industrial-policy proposal. However, if you are like most, should industrial policy become the law of the land, you will end up with less to say about those things that affect your lives.

If industrial policy prevails, George Orwell's big brother will take the form of a select, elitist council in Washington determining much of our economic way of life, including wages, prices, investments, and the allocation of national resources.

Some industrial-policy backers admit that a mishmash of red tape and federal edicts have thwarted efficiency in the U.S. economy. They say there was no single strategy behind the years of intervention by dozens of federal agencies.

True enough, but some of those same people (MIT economist Lester Thurow and New York banker Felix Rohatyn, to name two) then come out for *more* government intervention. Their reasoning seems to be that, since many small interventions over fifteen or twenty years didn't work, one huge intervention during the next few years will make things right.

There's as much wisdom in that as going on an ice-cream and chocolate-cake diet because the last one didn't help you lose weight.

Others favor an industrial policy to prevent what they call "deindustrialization." They paint a picture of nearly all America's manufactured products coming from overseas. This is scare-talk. According to Charles Schultze, who chaired the president's Council of Economic Advisers during the Carter-Mondale administration, U.S. deindustrialization is a myth.

"Throughout the industrial world, economic performance in the 1970s did fall behind the record of the 1960s," writes Schultze (now back with the Brookings Institution). "But relative to the industries of other countries, American industry performed quite well by almost all standards."

The key test of an economic policy, I believe, is job growth. Is the government, with low inflation and the correct regulatory and tax approach, creating an atmosphere in which the free market can create jobs?

In 1983, the American economy, after two years of falling inflation (and with tax cuts designed to remove the Carter-Mondale stag-flation which would've destroyed long-term job growth) began to deliver the goods. It added *four million new jobs.*

That's an average of 9,000 new jobs in every congressional district in the United States. No public-works scheme or industrial policy could deliver one-twentieth of that, even if every part of it worked flawlessly.

And it happened because of a Republican economic strategy using tax cuts and the free market, not because of a Democratic central planning approach based on controls and government loans.

In fact, the current recovery has seen a drop in unemployment of nearly three full percentage points—the greatest drop since the end of World War II.

Compare that trend with what's happening in Europe. All the countries there, democratic and communist alike, are well advanced on the big-government, industrial-policy route. (Switzerland is the one clear exception.) Here's what Newsweek said in its April 9, 1984, cover story on "The Decline of Europe":

Today, 1 out of 10 Europeans is unemployed. In Spain and the Netherlands the percentage is more than 17. And the shape of European joblessness is ugly, too. Four out of 10 unemployed people in the United Kingdom have been out of work for more than a year.

The cost of maintaining high unemployment payments and financing early retirements has put a strain on every European

136

udget. European governments boosted social outlays from 14 to 6 percent of their gross national products in the 1960s and 1970s. The corresponding increase in the United States was from 11 to 21 ercent...

No American should be happy at the plight of our sister emocracies in Europe. But neither should we be so mpathetic that we make the same mistakes they did.

It doesn't look like we're going to. Consider America's erformance as sketched by Grover Norquist of the U.S. Chamber of Commerce. He wrote in the Spring 1984 *Policy Review:*

America in the throes of a supply-sided recovery created more jobs n 1983 than Canada has created since 1965, four times as many obs as the British economy generated between 1950 and 1982, and s many jobs as Japan created in the entire decade of the 1970s.

All without an industrial policy—or the ultimately estructive high inflation and interest rates which went with ae job growth of the Carter-Mondale years.

Instead of adopting a national industrial policy, let's mphasize our strengths and stress *fundamentals.* A good nalogy, I believe, is a football team operating at less than ll capacity. Instead of trying to introduce spectacular ootball plays or entirely new offensive and defensive chemes to a team, a good coach will concentrate on basics— roper blocking, tackling, and conditioning. Until the ootball team masters these basics, it will have trouble unning any plays or defensive sets, no matter how ophisticated or new they may be.

The economic fundamentals for the United States include:
- improving the quality of our children's education
- improving our technically trained labor force

- increasing our savings and investment
- encouraging research and development
- reducing the size of the deficit and reforming the ta. code so that work and productivity are encouraged

What we really need to do is stay on a *high-growt. strategy.* The idea that we're in an "era of limits," that the pi is a big as it ever will be and therefore we must cut smalle and smaller pieces for people in our society, or cut large pieces for favored groups at the expense of others, is simpl wrong.

We must go with the traditional American thought that free marketplace can best expand that pie—can creat opportunities for *all* individuals, can provide an atmospher of incentive in which unshackled individual initiative encouraged and rewarded. That's what makes Americ great.

And that way we will bake an even larger pie—an without a big-brother government panel telling us how.

The Cliché

> *"Liberals are pro-education. Conservatives just want to cut budgets and lay off teachers."*

There is nothing fundamentally wrong with the American educational system. If more money needs to be spent, then liberals will spend it, because they're serious about making things better. Teacher groups like the National Education Association know who the friends of education are, and that's why NEA backs liberals and Democrats. The conservative approach to public education is out of date, anti-teacher, and obsessed with cutting costs.

14

What Would Really Improve Education?*

By Newt Gingrich, MC

The most important step in improving education today is not merit pay, tuition tax credits, or increased funds at any

---

* *This is from a chapter in Congressman Gingrich's forthcoming book,* Window of Opportunity: A Blueprint for the Future. *This book will be published by Baen Enterprises in cooperation with Tom Doherty Associates, and will be available from St. Martin's Press in August 1984.*

level. The most important step is to rethink the education process and system.

Woodrow Wilson once commented on the political tendencies of academic faculties. He said the United States Senate was far easier to deal with as president than the Princeton Senate was to deal with as president of Princeton University. Academicians may take pride in that comment but I don't think Wilson was referring to the intellectual prowess of the academic world.

The various education associations tend to be pork-barrel. In virtually every state, one of the most powerful, most narrowly focused and most money-oriented lobbies is the state teachers' association and/or union.

Part of the focus on money is defensive. Schoolteachers have been trapped by three major characteristics of their profession. First, as a profession less demanding than farming or heavy industry, education has historically been underpaid. Second, because public education is a manpower-intensive bureaucracy, the only avenues of additional salary have been politics and lobbying.

Third, education has remained a cottage industry: labor-intensive and capital-thin. Lacking the capital intensity and technological orientation of medical doctors, and lacking the political clout of lawyer-legislators simply to *coerce* the community, teachers became the most underpaid major profession.

The answer to this relative poverty within the big-government, liberal welfare-state philosophy is to organize more teachers, push harder for political muscle, and force higher wages for the same old services.

This is wrong for our children, our future generations, because it locks the education debate in a pork-barrel fight over money rather than a dialogue about the future of learning. It's wrong for the teachers because in the long run their profession has to change dramatically to become profitable. Organizing and unionizing force teachers in the wrong direction, especially when Americans are more and more dissatisfied with education-as-usual.

Let me suggest ten steps to improve significantly the state of education in America today.

1. Shift the focus of education from teaching to learning.

A *teacher*-focused system puts too much emphasis on the structure of academic disciplines and the bureaucratic lockstep of traditional classrooms, a nine-month school year, and annual promotions to higher grades.

No single group could be helped more by a focus on *learning* than poor children in the black community. Today's rewards are paper symbols designed in the narrowest sense to fit middle-class values. If you do well, you get a paper grade called an A. If you do badly, you get a paper grade called an F. All the while the numbers-runners, pimps, and drug dealers demonstrate *immediate* rewards for *their* type of behavior.

One experiment worth pursuing would be to offer a $500 bonus for any child who enters first grade reading at a fourth-grade level, so poor children and poor families would see a *real* advantage to achieving an excellence goal by a set deadline. If we combined that with an October "Achievement Sunday" in every local church, where the bonus-winners were recognized and could come down front, we'd have created a *joint social and economic reward system*. It would have real impact in poor communities and change the reading patterns of entire neighborhoods.

When children learn that basketball players may earn a million dollars, whereas studying only gets you a paper symbol, it's no wonder the summer is spent dribbling instead of reading. The tragedy is that few dribblers will make the National Basketball Association. If the same amount of energy were spent in learning marketable skills, the whole community would be far richer.

School authorities talk about age-grouping as a reason not to start children at a higher grade. But as long as children are told that what they learn is less relevant than how old they are, it should not surprise us that children believe learning is less important than bureaucratic rules.

If we made learning once again the prime focus of a public school system, we'd find many students learning very rapidly and leaving the system at a relatively early age. We'd find other students dropping out and getting jobs for a few years until they matured. Teachers could focus on designing learning experiences for the mid-level student who sincerely wants to learn but hasn't yet found the keys to knowledge on his or her own.

2. Promote lifetime learning and end assumptions about age.

As our culture and society change with new technology, new medicine, and new government rules, people will have to keep learning until they die. (One reason the liberal Democrats' demagogic 1982 campaign about social security worked was that so many senior citizens lacked adequate learning skills—they were easily frightened by *any* proposed change.)

We're all going to have to keep learning because whatever job we have today may not be the same as the job we will have in two years. Organized learning will become a key part of the unemployment compensation system, and people will be encouraged to moonlight at learning so they'll always be prepared if their job disappears or industry decays.

142

In addition, the shift from an industrial to an *information society* will make it both *easier* to learn and more profitable for those who *do* learn. The development of the home computer/cable television/telephone system/public library network will lead to an explosion of the knowledge available to average people right in their living room. Those citizens who keep learning will save money on their income tax, earn better incomes, buy better consumer goods, and travel further for less money.

3. Focus on discipline and the fundamentals.

Schools need to quit trying to be babysitter, social center, provider of ethical guidance, and introducer to dozens of interesting courses. The more things we've dumped on schools the less well they *do* any of them. Proliferation of objectives leads to decline in performance.

Schools need to return to setting priorities. They should then stick rigorously to those priorities until they are met. The two priorities for schools should be *basic mastery of the fundamentals* and the *development of social and academic discipline*.

We don't need to go back to the fundamentals of 1900. Instead we need to move forward to the "triliteracy" that best-selling author Alvin Toffler prescribes for our schools. Triliteracy combines reading, writing, and arithmetic with understanding of the mass media and computers.

Discipline can be taught partly in the classroom, but it's also the core reason for some extracurricular activities. Football, band, and any other endeavor which requires practice and determination, teach children how to carry on in adversity. (I learned a great deal of the discipline and pride which carried me through two losing congressional campaigns by playing football in high school.)

143

If a student is able to read and write, understand basic arithmetic, use a computer, and learn from the television and radio dealt with every day, he or she will have the core understanding and skills to build a flexible career in the future. If in addition the student has acquired self-discipline through a series of challenges, then a good citizen has been formed.

4. Move from state-focused teaching to society-supported learning.

We greatly underuse public libraries, newspapers, and TV channels: there are a host of learning opportunities in our society the education bureaucracy simply ignores.

We need a much closer relationship between the business community and education if America is to retain any kind of technological leadership in science and engineering. Most engineering schools and scientific laboratories simply can't afford modern equipment. Since in some fields there can be entire revolutions in technology every three or four years, it doesn't take many years for the laboratories to get out of date.

The result is school laboratories that resemble 1950 more than they do 1984. Many young engineers and scientists are trained on obsolete equipment. They must then be thoroughly retrained when they enter the business world and encounter modern equipment. We need legislation making it easy and profitable for businesses to share their investments in fine learning equipment with the academic world.

Furthermore, the bureaucratic model of education blocks people from contributing their talent to public learning. Our school employment rules are so stupid that a native German, who lacks education credits, would be barred from teaching

German, whereas a teacher who can't speak German but has all the necessary coursework, would be hired.

Finally, many decent citizens would be glad to help if only we could *organize* their participation. For instance, we could build a *senior citizens' volunteer corps* to help tutor students with particular problems. There are many grandparents with key skills and disciplines. At slight cost to society, some of these people would share their talents for two hours a week tutoring students who needed the personal touch.

5. Re establish apprenticeship systems.

One of the things keeping young poor people from breaking out of poverty has been the decline of *apprenticeship* systems. Good work habits and invisible assets such as building a network of contacts can be developed in an apprenticeship program more easily than in school.

Plus, many skills and trades are better learned in an apprenticeship than in a compartmentalized, academic environment. Cooking and politics, for example, are better learned from masters in action than in a classroom.

Finally, many young people simply don't fit well into school, but would be able to go to work, earn some money, and learn a trade.

A Conservative Opportunity Society would develop some experiments in apprenticeship, approve it as an alternative to high school, and offer tax advantages and subsidies to both the apprenticer and the community.

Of course, apprenticeship would be combined with a strong learner-focused program for all ages using the public library, home computers, television and radio programs, and a very extensive adult education system.

6. Experiment with mass media and computers for learning.

Today learning can be pursued with minimal inconvenience by people in hospital and nursing home beds; by mothers watching their children; by underemployed people who want to learn at night; and by people who just want to expand their knowledge for fun. For a modest sum we could build a computer software package that would make a large library available to your home computer by telephone hookup.

People with particular illnesses might take to learning from computer and videotape about the problems of their particular illness, the potential implications, and the correct way to take care of themselves. Or the government could use public television and direct mail to offer people in areas of high unemployment knowledge about how to get new jobs and learn new skills.

7. Challenge the mandarins of college life.

Today students study "political science" instead of either politics or government. *They study sociology instead of societies.* The academic world has become so self-important it thinks an introduction to the history of *its* ideas is the same as an introduction to the history of ideas *in general.*

Reality does not interfere with a typical social studies ("social science" is an arrogant misnomer) or education course. In these areas the student spends a great deal of time learning about the structure of knowledge rather than the structure of the world. In fact, the structure of knowledge *as taught* is merely the structure of the discipline and the student is taken further from reality.

The 1870s Harvard innovation of the modern undergraduate curriculum is ready for an overhaul. The 1880s

German invention of the modern Ph.D. program is equally ready for a clear challenge. It's time to look at different ways to organize knowledge and learning.

8. Move toward an intellectually open academe.

We still need someone to write the *Main Street* and *Babbitt* of academe. Babbitt's grandson is now a Ph.D. in Sociology. He earns a pittance, lives in genteel middle-class poverty, drives an old Volvo, and enjoys a Thursday afternoon wine-and-cheese party at a faculty member's home.

He feels morally superior to his high school classmates who entered business, medicine, or law. He knows they earn more than he does, but he *knows* more.

The left-wing ideological biases of the academic community are now as much a block to truth as were the right-wing biases of the community-at-large in the 1920s. The search for truth requires recognizing that there are *alternative* truths. But on many major campuses the only truth is left-wing.

The real debate we need is not just a question of Reagan politics versus McGovern-Mondale-Hart politics. We need an *intellectual* struggle in the academic community, not a *political* struggle.

Here are four specific questions for a true academic debate about American society:

1. Which ethnic groups in modern America have the color problems of the black community and rise anyway? Asiatic refugees, Chinese- and Japanese-Americans (including those uprooted in World War II), and West Indian blacks are ethnic minorities which seem to have risen faster than the black American community. What lessons can we learn, if that's true?

147

2. What are the lessons of the Vietnam War for the American use of power? Interestingly, most serious writing about the military history of Southeast Asia is coming from professional military theorists trying to form lessons for the future. The North Vietnamese have admitted they thought they had lost the 1968 Tet Offensive, that they consciously used the U.S. news media and the American left, and that they had planned the war in Hanoi and created the rebellion in South Vietnam as a front.

Yet, in spite of all that, the academic world still behaves as though Jane Fonda were right. A revisionist historical debate using the new data is badly needed.

3. What is the impact of the situation-ethics, hedonist-morality, left-wing bias of television as a mass entertainment medium? The reaction of the intellectual community would be violent if the evening entertainment were as biased toward Jerry Falwell's values as it is now biased against them.

4. How can we study economics in a way that takes into account interest-rate expectations, the entrepreneurial class's behavior, and the difference between societies that invent the future and those that import it? The current mode of economics is too mathematical, with an orientation toward the easily measured, the government-generated, and the statistically available.

The economy is more psychological and cultural than the current models admit, so much of our economic advice is closer to reading chicken bones than to serious science. Econometrics do not explain the rising prosperity of Hong Kong, Taiwan, Singapore, and South Korea. Orthodox economists were sure the West German free-market experiment of the late 1940 and would fail; it led to a boom instead.

Present economics, as management expert Peter Drucker

suggested, is only useful for linear projection of what we *already* know. All the big questions for society involve what we *don't* know.

This is just a sample of the kind of questions current biases prevent the academic community from studying properly.

9. Encourage people to read serious books without telling them they must become serious scholars.

One tragedy of the modern academic world has been its retreat from the true liberal arts education. People should be encouraged to learn about history so they know something about the world they live in. They should be encouraged to read fine fiction so they can learn more about themselves and about people in general.

Not only should a liberal arts education be for a lifetime, it should also *take* a lifetime. Benjamin Franklin established the American Philosophical Society in part so people would have a place to go and talk about *ideas*. We should encourage adults in every walk of life to take up the pursuit of ideas once again. Our goal should be that a generation from now the neighborhood recreation center would have an idea center as surely as it has a tennis center (and maybe even an "idea pro" to match the tennis pro).

10. Get our knowledge from action-research whenever possible.

Historian Lynn White notes that medieval agriculture progressed 1,500 years beyond contemporary medieval *academic* understanding of agriculture. Academicians were still reading Aristotle to learn about horses when there were modern horses on the hitching post outside their classroom.

Since medieval agriculture was making great breakthroughs in plowing and the use of the horse, it was the impractical man who listened to the academic.

We face a similar problem today. Too much of the academic world is tied up studying itself, and too little time is spent studying the world at large. Many more breakthroughs are being made in the world at large by practitioners than are being developed by academic intellectuals.

Especially in business, government, politics, and economics, we need to move back toward a reality-based approach to knowledge. Research in the real world must come before theoretical papers.

What you know and whether or not you are right should become as important as where you got a degree. Memoirs by first-grade teachers should be as academically important as analyses of questionnaires of first-grade teachers by intellectuals who've never taught first grade.

No single reform or set of reforms will adequately change the current system. The very effort to develop an "ideal national answer" will fail. What we need are thousands of experiments with computers, television, apprenticeships, voucher systems, action-research as a community resource, the business community's equipment and personnel, and especially the individual citizen who has *competence but no credentials.*

The data prove that we are the first generation in American history to educate our children less well than we were educated. Of the major Western nations we score close to the bottom in math and science. What we are doing is not working, *and we all know it.*

The structural innovations and attitude shifts I sketched will lead to some failures, but only by risking failure will we make great breakthroughs. We're looking for the Thomas Edisons and Henry Fords of learning. We'll find them more quickly if we make the atmosphere encouraging for entrepreneurs, innovators, and inventors.

What have we got to lose?

The Cliché

"A balanced-budget constitutional amendment is a bad idea, and a constitutional convention to write one is even worse."

Conservatives want to dodge blame for Reagan's big deficits by amending the U.S. Constitution to require balanced federal budgets. Since Congress has more important things to do, these conservatives are irresponsibly encouraging citizen groups in the states to call a constitutional convention to write the amendment. The convention would get out of control, tamper with the Bill of Rights, and jeopardize our oldest liberties. The Constitution is not the place to change economic policy, and a convention is not the place to change the Constitution.

15

Would a Balanced-Budget Amendment Work?

By Larry Craig, MC

The federal government has had only *one* balanced budget in the last twenty-four years. Deficit spending did not start with the Reagan administration or the Ninety-eighth Congress and it apparently will not end there either. It ha een a part of the federal spending system since most of ꞁday's policymakers were old enough to trade baseball ꞁrds.

It's evident that the nation's taxing and spending structure ꞁ not only badly flawed, but unworkable.

In reality, today's federal budgeting system is no ꞁudgeting system at all. There is one system of taxation for ꞁising revenues, and another for spending money. Spending ꞁ restrained only by occasional concern for how much red ꞁk must be used to stay in office. Silly as it seems, any real ꞁnk between spending money and raising money has ꞁmehow been lost.

In August 1982 the U.S. Senate passed and sent to the ꞁouse a proposed constitutional amendment to require ꞁalanced federal budgets and to limit taxes. It received a ꞁajority in the House, but fell forty-six votes shy of the two-ꞁirds required to send it to the states for ratification. Make ꞁ mistake about it, it was the same liberal leadership that ꞁchestrated the defeat of that amendment that is now crying ꞁe loudest about federal deficits.

Depending on the specific wording adopted, the ꞁnendment would limit federal spending to revenues expect ꞁhen three-fifths of Congress believe special circumstances ꞁquire deficit spending. It would cap tax increases by tying ꞁem to an index so balancing the budget is not an exercise in ꞁobbing wage-earning Peter to pay welfare-dependent ꞁaul." If passed, it would take a number of years for the ꞁnendment to become effective, giving Congress time to ꞁepare and adjust.

The Balanced-Budget/Tax-Limitation Amendment I've ꞁetched here is not the total answer to making Congress ꞁcally responsible. It does, however, offer the framework to ꞁrce the fundamental link between taxing and spending. It ꞁll force Congress to make the decisions regarding national

153

priorities that you and I grew up thinking it was supposed t
make. I grant that these will not be easy decisions to make
but it will make those who so easily spend our tax dollar
realize how hard those dollars are to come by.

Its simple passage would send signals to America
financial community that a *real* solution to the government
deficit-spending/debt dilemma is on the horizon. Th
economy would respond in earnest. Long-term economi
development would result as interest rates fall, no longe
remaining artificially high because of fear of inflation.

The masters of the tax-and-spend philosophy are now
part of a new breed of "born-again" fiscal conservative
outraged at the federal debt problem. But for all thei
shouting and finger-pointing at the White House, liberal
are doing all they can to prevent passage of the ver
structural changes necessary to confront effectively th
deficit-spending dilemma—a Balanced-Budget/Tax
Limitation Amendment to the U.S. Constitution.

Born-again fiscal chameleons defend their genera
opposition to, and defeat of, the balanced-budge
amendment by saying that "it isn't in the best interest of th
nation." The liberals would have us believe legislativ
solutions can take care of the problem, but one look at thei
legislative track record shows this solution is indeed part o
the problem. The Concurrent Resolution passed by th
House in June 1983 increased the deficit by $13 billion abov
President Reagan's requested level. Again, in Septembe
1983 the House passed the Wright amendment to HR 3913
which added $300 million to already overbudgeted Labor
Health and Human Services, and Education appropriation
bills.

Liberals know that legislative attempts to restrain federa
spending have failed over and over again because of the nee
to fulfill irresponsible and expensive campaign promises

Congress is caught between the welfare-state and special-interest-oriented constituencies it continues to finance on one hand, and the need to bring federal spending under control on the other. These benefit seekers focus intense lobbying efforts on narrow issues that, as single items, cost taxpayers little.

As the "unlimited" money pot swells, so does the circle of special-interest groups that demand their share. Today just about every American enjoys some type of federal benefit. Yet many Americans fail to recognize their portion of the American pie as part of the deficit-spending problem. It is always the other guy's program that should be cut. And Americans shouldn't believe otherwise when the congressional representative tells them they deserve more, not less. Congressional liberals, intent on not cutting off the ticket to reelection, talk not of *whether* to fund, but only of *how much*.

Reelection jitters have all but eliminated Congress's ability to deal with the problem. The system also compounds the problem. Congressional attempts to legislate balanced budgets have continually failed because one Congress cannot bind another, even by law. The next Congress faces the same pressures and unresolved problems as its predecessors. The annual budgets that Congress passes are nonbinding resolutions with little validity. It is a smokescreen the fiscal chameleons have used through three years of blaming someone else for spending too much or too little, whichever fits the circumstance.

When the time has come to end this charade and pass the Balanced-Budget/Tax-Limitation Amendment, liberals wrap themselves in the faulty arguments of a "constitutional crisis" and "congressional flexibility." If you remove all the clutter and cut through the verbiage liberals use to hide the truth, it boils down to their belief in the same big government, the same "Uncle Sam knows best" mentality that created our nation's current fiscal problems.

With the election of more Democrats to the House in 1982, the chances that Congress will pass a balanced-budget amendment on its own, without being forced to do so, got slimmer.

Fortunately for America, the Founding Fathers foresaw the time when the cozy congressional club would need to be shaken by the people. Article V of the U.S. Constitution "equally enables the state governments to originate amendments of errors," as James Madison put it. It provides that when two-thirds of the states petition Congress (through initiative or direct action by the legislatures), Congress must convene a constitutional convention to address the issue of the petitions.

In this case, that issue is the Balanced-Budget/Tax-Limitation Amendment.

The number of states needed to call the convention is thirty-four. The number having done so to date is thirty-two. Nine more states have passed the petition call through one house of their legislature. Four others have passed a balanced-budget resolution of support, but have not sent a formal petition to Congress.

For decades, public opinion polls have shown that a strong majority of Americans support the balanced-budget amendment. A June 1983 Gallup survey showed that, of those Americans at all familiar with the concept, over 70 percent favored the amendment.

Amendment opponents have subtly convinced the public that passage of the Balanced-Budget/Tax-Limitation Amendment is simply not going to happen because of insufficient support. They want people to think it is a lost cause. They're wrong.

At this point we confront the most impressive political

smokescreen of modern history. The liberals have spread so many stories about a "runaway constitutional convention dismantling the Constitution" and threatening the "very foundations of our Bill of Rights" that even those who should know better are beginning to think they are true. A letter signed by AFL-CIO President Lane Kirkland states, "We are concerned that upon application by thirty-four states, Congress may have no other choice but to convene a convention. And, once convened, a federal convention could well become an entity of its own, capable of contriving wholesale changes in the U.S. Constitution."

The late Senator Sam Ervin, a constitutional-law scholar, summed up this type of thinking: "The fear of a runaway convention is just a nonexistent constitutional ghost conjured up by people who are opposed to balancing the budget, because they want to be able to promise special groups something for nothing out of an empty pocket."

He is not alone in this view. Impartial experts in a two-year study by the American Bar Association unanimously said the same thing. Their official position: "Congress has the power to establish procedures limiting a convention to the subject matter which is stated in the applications received from the state legislatures."

Most state petitions to Congress specify consideration of only the Balanced-Budget/Tax-Limitation Amendment. The more recent petitions even include a "one last-chance" provision. These states provide that even if the thirty-four states required to force a convention do petition Congress, the convention should actually be called to order *only* if Congress fails to pass the amendment first. The parameters of the convention are clear. It cannot get out of control.

Beyond these legal opinions and state-imposed restrictions lie the provisions of the Constitution itself. Here, Congress is given the power to set the rules for the convention, including delegate selection, convention location, and delegate compensation.

Congressional liberals who hide behind the fear of a runaway convention are afraid either of themselves or of the balanced-budget amendment. The reasons are easy to see.

In short, there are multiple checks placed on the convention method to prevent it from covering anything but what the states intended—the Balanced-Budget/Tax-Limitation Amendment. The final check, however, is that no matter what the convention devises, it must *still be ratified by three-fourths of the states* to be part of the Constitution.

Common sense tells us that if congressional liberals really believed their drivel about a runaway convention, they would send an amendment of their own to the states, let the people decide, and avert the convention altogether. Period. And that strikes at the very heart of this whole constitutional-crisis, antiamendment smokescreen. These "born-again" fiscal chameleons have so disguised the truth in seemingly genuine concern for the nation and the Constitution that the truth almost gets lost. That is just what they intend. The liberals won't pass the balanced-budget amendment to the states because they do not want to enact a balanced-budget amendment or limit taxes.

It became obvious to me that there must be a great many others who, like me, are frustrated with the arrogance of the liberal House leaders and their indifference to the wishes of the people. I knew there had to be a lobby that represents the taxpayers and indeed national organizations do exist. These groups are in states that have not petitioned Congress to enact an amendment. They seek to organize initiatives or lobby legislatures in behalf of the amendment.

Unfortunately, the liberal misinformation has been working as well. The Balanced-Budget/Tax-Limitation Amendment cause has lost some steam in recent years. Of the thirty-two states petitioning Congress, thirty did so before 1979.

The AFL-CIO has taken it upon itself to lead the counteroffensive. The union leaders might not have the support of their rank and file, but they have a list of some fifty organizations that reads like a who's who in American left-wing politics, including the American Civil Liberties Union, Common Cause, and the NAACP.

The AFL-CIO propaganda campaign provides us with a simple summary of the type of emotionalism the liberals are using to drum up opposition to the balanced-budget amendment. The liberals tell us that enactment of the amendment would reduce health, veterans', and education benefits by over 70 percent. They assert it would ruin social security, destroy transportation programs, and virtually ensure an immediate national depression. And, of course, the ultimate evil, a constitutional crisis.

Below the surface of these absurd and crude statements lies a very active campaign. Its intent is to prevent any more states from petitioning Congress, and to pressure some that did to rescind it.

In November 1983, having had about all the propaganda I could take and frustrated at not being able to work within the congressional system to get real change, I formed my own CLUBB. Congressional Leaders United for a Balanced Budget is composed of congressmen who are dedicated to assisting the proamendment national organizations in getting the two states to force Congress to act on the amendment.

In the months ahead, we are willing to go to California, Washington, Ohio, Montana, Kentucky, or other targeted states to drum up support. We will appear alone or in teams before large groups, small groups, and state legislatures.

In every case our message will be the same: the nation

159

needs to enact the balanced-budget/tax-limitation amendment. There is no effective alternative. If Congress won't do it, the people must.

Government will never be the substitute for the people. Indeed, our living Constitution was devised for that reason. In the end, the only real freedom we have is the freedom to discipline ourselves.

It is very doubtful that a convention will be convened. In 1911, the U.S. came *within one state* of its first constitutional convention since 1787. Then the issue was the direct election of U.S. senators. Before that, they were appointed by state legislatures. When the people seriously threatened to call the convention, Congress finally broke up that cozy political arrangement and sent the Seventeenth Amendment to the states for ratification, and senators were elected by the people.

I doubt the liberal House leaders will act any differently in this case. The thought of losing power to delegates at a convention spreads more fear within them than the thought of the amendment.

When I encounter arguments against balancing the federal budget and limiting taxes, I remember Thomas Jefferson's words:

I place economy among the first and most important virtues and public debt as the greatest of dangers. To preserve our independence, we must not let our rulers load us with perpetual debt. We must make our choice between economy and liberty, or profusion and servitude. If we can prevent the government from wasting the labors of the people under the guise of caring for them, they will be happy.

One last thought: Liberals say the Constitution isn't the place to make economic policy. Remind them that the

Sixteenth Amendment gave Congress "the power to lay and collect taxes on incomes." Why do liberals approve of the constitutional amendment empowering the government to tax incomes, but disapprove of an amendment limiting government spending?

Finally, *you can help* our nationwide effort to make the Balanced-Budget/Tax-Limitation Amendment a part of the Constitution. Write letters to the editor of your hometown newspaper. Write national associations and organizations to which you belong and encourage them to adopt a national resolution supporting a balanced-budget amendment. Contact your state legislators and let them know you support the amendment. Talk with your friends, neighbors, and relatives on the merits of a balanced-budget amendment.

It is only a matter of time before our goal becomes a reality. The sooner we cause it to happen, the sooner we can control the irresponsibile spending habits of Congress. If we fail to act now, our children and grandchildren will be crushed by government debt. Their dreams will never have the opportunity to become reality and their future will be controlled by an elite establishment sitting comfortably on the Hill in Washington, D.C.